CAREERS IN SOCIAL SERVICE

Work in social service covers the entire spectrum of human need. In city slums, rural poverty belts and new suburban communities, in hospitals and clinics, in institutions for the old, the young and those gone astray, there is an urgent demand for dedicated young men and women who find fulfillment in helping others. This book shows the vast scope of modern social service, under the authority of federal, state or local government, church institutions and private foundations. It covers the educational requirements, special skills, desirable personality traits and attitudes for careers in a challenging field that offers immense rewards for those concerned with the multitude of human problems in today's complex world.

BOOKS BY KATHLYN GAY

BETH DONNIS: Speech Therapist

CAREERS IN SOCIAL SERVICE

GIRL PILOT

KATHLYN GAY

CAREERS IN SOCIAL SERVICE

Illustrated with Photographs

Julian Messner
New York

361.0623
G 25c
68705
February, 1970

ACKNOWLEDGMENTS

A book covering such a broad field as social service could not be written without the help and guidance of many people. I am especially grateful to Mrs. Jeanette Hanford, Director, Family Service Bureau, Chicago; Charles G. Chakerian, Ph.D., McCormick Theological Seminary, Chicago; Elias Picheny, Administrative Field Secretary, Jewish Welfare Board, Chicago; Lester Glick, Ph.D., Goshen College, Goshen, Indiana; Catherine S. Guyler, Director, National Commission for Social Work Careers, New York, for the extraordinary amount of time they contributed for interviews or special assistance.

Mrs. E. M. Reid, Director, Social Work Careers Project, Oakland, California; Mrs. Carolyn Selling, Director, Social Work Careers in Oregon; Mrs. Jane L. Falender, Central Services Associate, Community Service Council of Metropolitan Indianapolis, Inc.; Katherine Daly, Field Consultant, Florence Crittenton Association of America, Inc., also put forth considerable effort to help with this book.

Thanks are also due to: Sister Maria Mercedes, S.S. N.D., Director of Information and Research, National Conference of Catholic Charities, Washington, D. C.; Jean Illiovici, Chief, Social Welfare Ser-

vices Section, United Nations; John LaHoud, Public
Information, Peace Corps, Washington, D. C.; Mrs.
Charles S. Monroe, Executive Secretary, Depart-
ment of Christian Social Relations, Episcopal
Church, N. Y.; Mrs. Lois M. Dussler, Administra-
tive Assistant, National Presbyterian Health and
Welfare Association, N. Y.; Henry B. Stern, Per-
sonnel Services, National Jewish Welfare Board,
N. Y.; S. Norman Feingold, National Director,
B'nai B'rith Vocational Service, Washington, D. C.;
Wilson Radway, Special Projects Director, Church
World Service, N. Y.; Mary R. Baker, Director of
Personnel Service, Family Service Association of
America, N. Y.; Norman A. Durfee, National Direc-
tor, American National Red Cross, Washington,
D. C.; Imogene M. Huffman, Recruitment and Em-
ployment Coordinator, American National Red
Cross, Washington D. C.; Mrs. Mary Fry, Director
of Public Relations, Travelers Aid Association,
N. Y.; William T. Parker, Assistant Chief, Tech-
nical Liaison Office, Department of the Army, Washington, D. C.; Delwin M. Anderson, Director, Social
Work Service, Veterans Administration, Washington, D. C.; Milton Wittman, D.S.W., Chief, Social
Work Training Branch, Department Health, Education and Welfare, Chevy Chase, Maryland; William
D. Gray, Visual Information Specialist, Department
of Health, Education and Welfare, Social & Rehabilitation Service, Washington, D. C.; Cordelia Cox,

Bureau of Family Affairs, Washington, D. C.; Leonard A. Tropin, Director of Public Education, National Council on Crime and Delinquency, N. Y.; Daniel O'Connor, Director, Information Department, American Foundation for the Blind, Inc,; Charles G. Muller, United Community Funds and Councils of America, Inc., N. Y.

In the field of youth and recreation services the following people provided valuable information: Frances J. Rotundo, Director of Personnel Administration, Camp Fire Girls, Inc., N. Y.; August Howard, Public Relations, Boy Scouts of America, New Brunswick, N. J.; William J. Lavery, Associate Director, Personnel and Training Service, Boys' Clubs of America; Martha May Newsom, National Field Service Director, Girls Clubs of America, Inc., N. Y.; Jane McAfee, Personnel Consultant, YWCA, N. Y.; Gordon H. Mack, Director of Recruiting, YMCA, N. Y.; W. C. Sutherland, Director, Educational Services, National Recreation and Park Association, Washington, D. C.

Directors of many social-work-careers programs provided special assistance, and I am grateful to: Patricia Leonard, Chicago; John G. Geist, Baltimore; Mrs. Hope G. Murrow, Boston; Louis Levitt, New York; Mrs. Burdett Wylie, Cleveland; Robert S. Jones, Miami, Florida; Mary Alice Messerley, St. Louis; Marjorie E. Battersby, Los Angeles; Mrs. Helen B. Humphrey, Cincinnati; Katrine Nickel,

Pittsburgh; Stanley L. Laine, St. Paul, Minnesota; Mrs. Marilyn H. Brown, New Brunswick, N. J.

Of utmost importance in a book of this kind is the knowledge and insight gained by being able to share the day-by-day experiences of professional social workers: Robert Pollitt, Charles Burkholder, Mike Thompson, William MacDonough, Glen Good, Nancy Outley, Mrs. Goldie Ivory, Mrs. Virginia Nortdurf, Mrs. Charlene Imhoff of the South Bend–Elkhart, Indiana area. Thank you.

If I have failed to acknowledge any person who has contributed to this manuscript, it is unintentional.

—K.G.

CONTENTS

CONTENTS

1
SOCIAL SERVICE— THE HUGE UMBRELLA

If you had a TV camera with a lens powerful enough to pan the country and zoom in on people performing the many kinds of social services that are available, the scenes recorded would be multitudinous. Your camera would bring to the viewing screen thousands of men and women who have chosen careers that are concerned with the development of individual potential and the fulfilling of needs of many kinds.

Focus for a minute on New York City's Department of Social Services, where Paula Smith sits at a desk interviewing clients who need aid in the form of a winter coat, a washing machine, baby clothes or a larger monthly allotment check. Helping clients determine whether or not they are eligible for such services is only part of Mrs. Smith's job, and she is only one of a staff of over six thousand case workers.

Another social-service career worker has her desk at the Traveler's Aid booth in Chicago's Union Station. Mrs. Betty Gordon is director of the professional staff for the Traveler's Aid Society in that city, which provides on-the-spot counseling for juveniles who have run away from home, or such services as financial assistance for stranded travelers and, in emergencies such as a recent major railroad strike, the direction of people to other means of transportation.

Pan to the Illinois State Training School at St. Charles, where some eight-hundred delinquent boys have been committed to the largest correctional institution of its kind in the United States. The school's superintendent, Samuel Sublett, is a career man. He heads up a staff that provides counseling on personal problems, vocational training, psychological testing, recreational programs and other services. The ultimate goal: rehabilitating boys to be productive young men, rather than destructive forces in society.

Some 2,500 miles west, Bernard Mayes sits at a desk in the San Francisco Suicide Prevention office. Mayes is the director of this social service agency, which has a staff of one hundred to answer over thirteen hundred calls a month from potential suicide victims. The desperate who dial the well-publicized SFSP number are persuaded to identify themselves and their locations, then are soothed, coaxed, literally talked out of attempts to kill themselves. An ambulance might be sent or a doctor rushed to the scene to give further aid, and, if possible, psychiatric counseling is arranged through another agency.

In Stockton, California, Prof. William Byron, a social worker–educator, is heading up an experimental program for delinquent boys under the auspices of the University of the Pacific. Volunteer university students, who are thoroughly screened to weed out the "merely curious or *casual* do-gooder," serve as staff for Byron's rehabilitation program in a state school for boys near Stockton. The students work with hard-core delinquents in group projects, are able to communicate in across-the-table talks during meals in wards and plan social activities such as occasional dances and group sings. Successful results can be seen in formerly hostile inmates who now say, "I understand people better. . . . I'm sure I'll make it on the streets when I get out."

Down the coast in a Southern California town, a social worker employed by the local Council of Churches is counseling families of migrants—people who "travel with the crops," cultivating fields of truck produce or picking fruit during the growing and harvesting seasons. These families may need financial assistance or health services, or may need to be shown the value of using the educational services that are available for their children.

13

Back in the Midwest, Julio Rivera is a social worker, with the title "Program Director for Youth and Adults," in the YMCA of a medium-sized town. With a nearly completed master's degree in social work, Rivera is able to handle a wide range of duties: guiding a belligerent boy into cooperative recreational activities; counseling an alcoholic who has taken refuge in the Y's dorm; arranging night classes for a group of adults who want to further their education.

Dolly-in on an Indiana city where Goldie Ivory is a social worker. Called a supervisor of attendance and social services, Mrs. Ivory works in the public-school setting, but her job takes her to many places and includes many duties, such as meeting with an interracial group that is an outgrowth of a Head Start program; buying shoes out of a school fund for a needy child; making calls on parents whose children have behavior problems.

Now spot-check such diverse places as Madison, Wisconsin, Cincinnati, Ohio, Utica, New York, and many other cities across the nation. You will find a working force of women who are part of the homemaker services connected with departments of welfare or private agencies. These trained women are sent, under agency supervision, to homes where a mother's absence may be shattering a child's security; where the mother may be bedridden by illness; where a panic-stricken teen-age mother may lack basic understanding of how to care for her infant.

Zoom around the world—and come in on Pax workers (volunteers in a Mennonite social-service program) who are establishing agricultural programs, constructing schools and working on other community projects in such places as India, Vietnam, Haiti, Algeria.

And in the Philippines, Peace Corps volunteer Ed Luker helps villagers construct a rice-threshing machine from a hollowed-out log, a saving of both time and effort for farmers and their families, who previously prepared the rice with mortar and pestle.

Put all of these pictures together, and you still have only a few of the jobs and areas of work in social service. Generally speaking, social service might also include nursing, teaching, the ministry and other professions that help people and improve society as a whole. But the term "social service" as it is being used here covers more specific kinds of work, plus special organizations and agencies equipped to prevent and treat a variety of social problems. Even so, our definition of social service covers a broad area. You will want to have close-up studies as well as panoramic views to help you decide whether this is the career field in which you belong.

The variety of work available in social service is a relatively new phenomenon, although charitable acts and some type of organized aid for "unfortunates" have always been part of our Judeo-Christian tradition. In fact, services that helped individuals meet their basic needs have been part of most cultures from ancient times to the present.

However, circumstances, technology and resources available in each period of history have brought different approaches and change. The social worker of the present decade is a far cry from the Overseer of the Poor of colonial times or the wealthy matron of the last century who dispensed cheerful smiles and sometimes baskets of food to destitute families. Our modern hospitals and homes for rehabilitating the disadvantaged attempt to help individuals, rather then herd the orphaned, mentally ill and other "misfits" into institutions, merely to get them out of the way and keep them from "contaminating" the rest of society.

There are still social institutions and conditions in society today that require changes and improvement. And there are many health and welfare problems that must be solved. Possibly you will be a part of a dramatic, banner-waving reform movement. But not all social workers can be involved in social *action*— that is, broad, sweeping revolutions. However, it is certain that if social service is your career choice, you will have a hand in changes and improvements in individuals, families and/or groups and communities.

We have come a long way from handouts and condescending charity to a recognition that all people have social needs. Government, business and individuals are asking, *"What* should be done and *who* should accept the responsibility for providing economic security, emotional stability, 'the good life' for all?"

A 1965 Task Force Report for the U.S. Department of Health, Education and Welfare points out that in the present century "an organized system of methods and techniques and a variety of defined services" have evolved under the term "social work," and these are "designed to enable individuals, groups and communities to meet their needs and solve their problems of adjustment to a changing pattern of society and through cooperative action to improve economic and social conditions."

Thus social work has become a profession—and its practitioners apply knowledge from physical, social and behavioral sciences based on theory and tested experience. Professional social workers, and others who are career people in social service, usually work as employees of agencies or institutions.

If you were job hunting today for a position in social service, you would have a choice of several types of "employers."

There are *public or tax-supported programs* and institutions. These include school systems, state and county welfare departments and antipoverty programs which hire people of various levels of skill in social work. In addition, there is work with veterans and the military, the probation and parole offices of the courts, corrective institutions, housing developments and programs for the aged.

Private agencies—supported by voluntary contributions—employ social workers. Family-service agencies, adult and child guidance centers, chapters of the Red Cross, Girl and Boy Scouts, Jewish community centers, settlement houses, Traveler's Aid Societies, centers for retarded children, some mental health clinics and day-care centers are just a few of the many such agencies.

There are also *religiously oriented organizations,* or agencies sponsored by religious groups, which offer careers in social service. The YM-YWCA are examples. Agencies associated with the National Conference of Catholic Charities, National Presbyterian Health and Welfare Association, Department of Christian Social Relations of the Episcopal Church, the Board of Social Ministry of the Lutheran Church in America (one of the major Lutheran groups), the Mennonite Board of Missions and Charities are others. There are also some religiously motivated Jewish agencies—but none is under the auspices of synagogue or temple, nor is there a national coordinating body.

Finally, you might be employed by *overseas or international agencies* such as the Peace Corps, Church World Service, Catholic Relief Services, American Friends Service Committee, the Unitarian-

18

Universalist Service Committee, Lutheran World Relief, the American Jewish Joint Distribution Committee, AID (Agency for International Development), CARE and programs of the United Nations. The primary concern of overseas social workers is the improvement of community life and living conditions in developing countries.

Community improvement is also an important type of service rendered by social workers in the United States. *Group work* and individual and family *casework* are the other two general types of service provided. There are many job variations within the three categories. Some are on the professional level, and require a master's degree in social work. There are also many opportunities for college graduates with a good foundation in social sciences. And if you don't complete a college education, there are career jobs that are comparable to those of medical and dental technicians or assistants.

Studies of career opportunities in social work have been conducted by the National Commission for Social Work Careers and affiliated state programs, by universities, by state departments of health, by welfare associations of religious bodies and many others. All investigations reveal that the demand for social workers is far beyond the present supply of qualified personnel. Some reports show that at least twenty-thousand *new* social workers will be needed annually to fill vacancies through the 1970's.

If you graduate from a school of social work accredited by the Council on Social Work Education, you can expect a starting salary of from $8,000 to $9,500 per year and up to $18,000 after ten years experience. Some top jobs may pay up to $25,000 or even $35,000 annually. Without an advanced degree, annual pay starts at $5,000 to $7,500 and does not rise as rapidly.

While salaries are steadily improving, you can see you won't get rich in this field. However, if you are like most people who go into social service as a career, money—important as it is—will not be the only compensation you will receive. Self-fulfillment is often one of the rewards for helping others improve their lives, and it is exciting to be part of a career group that helps influence and carry out programs that are set up on the ideals of justice and equality of opportunity for all.

The challenge is there. But now you will want to learn what personal qualifications are especially valuable for anyone planning a career in social service.

2
ARE YOU A DO-GOODER?

It wasn't too many years ago that almost anyone who made a career of aiding the economically destitute and the socially handicapped was referred to as a "do-gooder." The term was far from complimentary, and it immediately brought to mind a picture of a rather stocky, granite-faced woman of indeterminate age. Wearing coarse stockings and heavy-heeled shoes and carrying a satchel, she would march with righteous determination across the tracks to do her duty. In the stereotyped version, that duty included a lecture on moral weaknesses or inspirational preachings along with whatever material aid was doled out.

This notion of an indignant, holier-than-thou worker intent on doing "good" to and for others—

whether they liked it or not—has not completely disappeared. Partly this is due to characterizations in novels and films which have popularized the caricature of the social worker.

The movies of the thirties, for example, often included a snoopy "welfare worker" whose main function seemed to be that of putting obstacles in the way of the young heroine's happiness—all in the name of "rightness" and "goodness." Some films and stories showed heroes and heroines encountering spinsters from the "welfare" who provided the conflict for the plot instead of a means to a happy ending.

Even the play *A Thousand Clowns,* which ran on Broadway in 1962 and was adapted a few years later for a movie, includes a straight-laced social worker and her supervisor who live by the rule book, sit in judgment and seem to have little sympathy for human frailties—until the plot begins to unravel.

This picture of a part-villainous, part-omnipotent person, who makes a habit of spying on the downtrodden, is in most instances an unfair portrayal of the social worker's role. Yet, there is *some* justification for this interpretation.

Historically, it had its beginnings in colonial America of the 1600's, long before there were social workers as such or highly organized social services.

Since many of the colonists who helped settle the early communities of this country were from England, they brought with them British customs and ideas, as well as laws and institutions. The self-sufficient settlers, especially in New England, carried with them the attitudes prevalent in England. They believed that if a man worked hard, was thrifty and behaved according to a strict religious code, material success was bound to come. Idleness was considered a sin. Thus, poverty and unhappiness had to be caused by immorality and laziness. It followed also that paupers and beggars were the next thing to criminals —if not actually labeled as such.

Along with this concept, the colonists believed in taking care of their own, giving assistance when needed in time of trouble to family members or to close neighbors. If a person had no relatives or friends to care for him when illness struck or there was financial distress, he might be able to get some help from the church—providing he was a member in good standing. Or possibly he would receive a very meagre "outdoor relief," from the town—that is, food, fuel and clothing sent to the home and provided by a "poor tax."

However, there was little extra money or material goods in these early communities to support public-assistance programs. Families were struggling just to survive. This lack of abundance and the contempt for poverty combined to set the standards and laws for treatment of people in need.

Everything possible was done to discourage poverty and to repress individuals who might be inflicted with this "disease"; but the number of paupers increased as the population increased. In the larger cities, colonists set up workhouses for the poor, patterned after the English almshouses established in accordance with the Elizabethan Poor Law of 1601, which first outlined the responsibility of government to provide some aid for people who could not maintain themselves.

But, just as in England, the workhouses or poorhouses of this country from colonial times through the nineteenth century were hardly humane. Often orphans, old people, the insane, the sick and people with all kinds of handicaps who had no means of support were thrown together in run-down buildings. Many of these dependents were forced to perform hard labor under the rigid discipline of a superintendent. In return they received food, clothing and a roof over their heads—but they seldom lived as well as domestic animals.

In the smaller towns the poor, the widows and the sick would be "farmed out"—placed wherever they would be accepted at the least expense to the town. And it was common practice to indenture orphans or children who had been abandoned by their parents. This meant children were put in foster homes and worked for their keep, serving as apprentices or as farm laborers until they were adults.

Needy people who were not permanent residents of

a community, such as immigrants and wanderers, were severely punished for their "crime" of impoverishment, regardless of the circumstances which had caused their condition. Such persons were whipped, then deported or sent out of town.

Again, this kind of treatment was a carry-over of the attitude that a pauper or anyone in distress who could not help himself was getting his just due.

The development of social services in this country had a circuitous history, with periods of decline as well as advancement, which is too complex to cover in a few brief paragraphs. But the demand for such services was keenly felt after the Civil war.

In the fifty years from 1860 to 1910, the population increased by 61 million—a rate of growth which had never been known before. In addition, there was also a tremendous increase in mobility, with people leaving the farms and moving to the cities. The rapid increase in population, adjustment to urban life and expanding industrialization, plus an unstable economy and many other factors, combined to cause myriad social problems. Poverty, miserable working and living conditions for the majority, child labor, underlying insecurity were prevalent.

At first, attempts to cope with these problems were chaotic and haphazard, and there was still the tendency to blame low morals for all kinds of social ills and to segregate the "undeserving" elements. Yet there were dedicated reformers who were motivated by concern for individuals no matter what their background and environment.

Dorothea Dix is a well-known example. In 1841 she began her work to eradicate the deplorable housing of the insane and mentally deficient who were chained to walls or put in cold cellars, cages or stalls. Nearly every text on social work and social welfare describes how she almost singlehandedly began a crusade to improve the treatment of these and other unfortunates. As a result, state hospitals for the insane were established, and prisoners and people in county poorhouses were treated more humanely.

Around this same period, Dr. Samuel Gridley Howe, a Harvard Medical School graduate, and Dr. John D. Fisher, a Boston physician, were establishing the Massachusetts Asylum for the Blind in Boston. Both men had observed and studied methods for educating the blind in Europe, and their asylum, which eventually was called a School for the Blind, had outstanding successes—especially as personified by a blind and deaf girl, Laura Bridgman. Dr. Howe taught the girl, who had been considered a hopeless idiot for seventeen years, to read and speak, and she developed into an intelligent, productive woman.

During the year 1899, Jane Addams established Hull House in Chicago. The story of this famous social settlement and its founder inspired many people to go into careers in social work. With a friend,

Jane Addams took over an elegant mansion which had been sold because it was located in a neighborhood that was rapidly turning into a slum.

Patterned after London's Toynbee Hall, the first settlement house in the world, the mansion became a service center for thousands of immigrants in the area. Employment bureaus, adult-education classes and day care for children were just a few of the services offered in the early days of Hull House. All through her career, Jane Addams constantly sought ways to help people better their lives and live peaceably with those of other races, religions and nationalities.

These people, and many others, helped to formulate the concepts and principles basic to the social-work profession and the health and family services provided today. They were not all called social workers or social service practitioners, but they would be comparable to the modern career persons in social services who, according to the National Association of Social Workers, "seek to reduce human wastage [and] enable people to live more productively, wipe out festering problems—delinquency, family disintegration, poverty, unprotected old age . . . assist people of all ages to uncover and deal with hampering problems that have arisen within themselves, in their families, or in their life situations . . . to enlarge their horizons and set their lives in constructive directions."

This type of modern social worker is more than a descriptive set of words. And his influence was apparent in a recent television series, "East Side/West Side." George C. Scott played the social-service worker who dealt with everything from drug addiction to the problems of families living in slum areas. The drama's emphasis was always on the individual who needed help to understand himself, and to set his life in "constructive directions."

In this television production the term "do-gooder" was not a label of which to be ashamed. And many magazines and newspapers now contain stories about real people with similar qualities who are involved in social services of which they are proud to be a part.

Take for example Judy Lewis, a VISTA (Volunteers in Service to America) volunteer on Harlem's 118th Street during the summer of 1966. In an interview with *Look Magazine,* she talked about helping people in the slums "want to change, try to change." She was thoroughly involved in the block work— getting neighbors to work together for community improvement. She said she was able to "connect" with most of the 320 families on her block so that they became committed to the idea of improvement. As the reporter described it: "Judy Lewis doesn't pity the poor, she bugs them. She is no preachy charity pusher, with a helping hand that holds people down. . . ." Like many other VISTAs in the sick

28

parts of cities, she was "close enough to make contact, touch people" not just problems.

In a Chicago daily, a recent headline proclaimed: "TRI-FAITH SERVICE FINDING JOBS FOR GHETTO WORKERS." Monroe B. Sullivan, executive director of the agency, and his staff are professional social workers who are justly proud of that headline and can show proof of how their kind of social service meets specific needs. Sponsored by Federal funds and Catholic, Jewish and Protestant organizations, the agency finds employment for low-skilled, deprived people in the city. The Tri-Faith Employment Service has seven offices in depressed areas of Chicago. Although it is a relatively small agency, it has an impressive record of placement. Those applying for jobs may also get help with housing, medical care and other needs through appropriate agencies to which they have been referred by Sullivan and his staff.

Then there's the story that made the newspaper wire services: A New York mother of two, a divorcee who was once a welfare recipient, managed to get through college so that she herself could be a social worker. She is now a hospital caseworker and says, "I believe I can help people who must have public assistance, because I can understand how people on relief feel."

Empathy—being able to feel as others feel—and

determination to acquire the required educational background are just two of the characteristics you should have if you plan a career in social services. In fact, a liking for people and an interest in their problems, as well as those of society as a whole, plus a better-than-average intelligence, are qualities that should be a basic part of your makeup.

Because your personality and attitudes are in many ways inseparable from the techniques you will learn in the helping process, it is extremely important, as you think about this career, to make an honest appraisal of yourself.

For one thing, you should be able to say with a reasonable amount of certainty that you know your own weaknesses as well as your strengths. You should be learning to build on and develop your strengths rather than giving in to the less constructive side of your personality. This trait is essential for any kind of productive life, and for a would-be social-service worker it is especially important to understand both the positive and negative (or the "good" and "bad") sides of oneself. Later you will need to see these factors at work in others and to be able to help them put their productive qualities to best use.

This suggests several other qualities you should have: tolerance, patience, flexibility, awareness and sensitivity. These qualities will help you develop certain *abilities* needed in social services.

For example, if you are tolerant, you will be able to listen to and accept points of view different from your own. And you will not sit in judgment—condemn people for ideas or behavior which you may regard as "vulgar" or even immoral.

If you are patient, you will be able to accept the fact that productive change in people sometimes takes a long time.

If you are flexible, you will be able to work harmoniously with others and will be able to take suggestions and advice, or, if necessary, adapt to someone else's way of doing things. You will also have the ability to help strangers adapt to unfamiliar or difficult situations.

If you are aware and sensitive, you will be considerate of others' feelings. And you will also have your antenna out—be tuned in—to catch unspoken bits of information about a person or pleas for help which may not be verbalized.

More aggressive characteristics are also necessary. Perseverance, objectivity, initiative, creativity, strong personal convictions and the ability to organize are all qualifications you should develop if they are not already a part of your personal assets.

Underlying all of this should be a positive attitude that life is worth living, so that you have a healthy curiosity, a variety of interests and a sense of humor. For balance, you will need to bring a certain amount of levity to your work with people in distress, because there can be a lighter side to even the most difficult problems.

For other ideas about personal qualifications and aptitudes, be sure to read chapters pertaining to this in career books that you will find in your public library. Here are a few:

Beck, Bertram S., *Your Future in Social Work.* New York: Richards Rosen Press, Inc., 1964.

Koestler, Frances A., *Careers in Social Work.* New York: Henry Z. Walck, Inc., 1965.

Paradis, Adrian A., *Toward a Better World: the Growth and Challenge of Social Service.* New York: David McKay Co., 1966.

Perlman, Helen Harris, *So You Want to Be a Social Worker.* New York: Harper & Row, 1962.

Williamson, Margaret, *Social Worker: Artist and Scientist in Human Relations.* New York: Macmillan Co., 1964.

Also, the National Commission on Social Work Careers has a concise career chart listing personal aptitudes, educational requirements and job opportunities. You can obtain the chart by enclosing twenty-five cents with your request to NCSWC, 2 Park Avenue, New York, New York.

Your high-school counselor can help you secure many pamphlets, booklets and other published materials on careers in social services. The professional staff people in public and private social-service agencies will be able to explain the nature of the work, especially as it pertains to their specific agencies.

During your high-school years, you can also test your aptitudes by doing volunteer work. For example, summer church and Y camps may offer opportunities to assist younger children in group projects, guiding them and helping them work together. Maybe you are already on a student-government council or in a club or other organization that can help you determine how well you get along with people. Canvassing for a United Fund drive or working for other worthwhile causes will also help you get a taste of what social services are all about.

These suggestions are only "teasers." If you decide upon social service as a career, you have a long road ahead, and there is no sense trying to gloss over the fact. But that shouldn't discourage you. Your interest in social services is more than a passing fancy by now, isn't it? Then take a deep breath and go on.

3
BEING A PROFESSIONAL

When I first got into social work, I thought I understood what it was all about," says Charles Burkholder, who directs a family counseling service in the Midwest. "My wife and I were eager to help the adolescent boys for whom we were house parents in a public institution for delinquents. But we soon found out it took more than our good intentions and sympathy to help them. We had never known any problem kids before and had no background in behavioral sciences. So I decided to go back to the university for graduate work—that was over twelve years ago. . . ."

Today, Charles Burkholder has his master's degree in social work and a good deal of experience as a practitioner in various social-service settings. He holds a responsible position as an executive, supervising other professionals on his counseling staff. And often, on the correspondence he dictates each week, he signs his name over the initials A.C.S.W. The privilege of using these initials is accorded to a relatively small group of some 29,000 of the more than 125,000 social-work practitioners in this country. The initials stand for "Academy of Certified Social Workers."

To be admitted to the academy, you have to meet prescribed standards of a national certification program. These standards include a master's degree in social work plus two years experience in one agency under the supervision of an academy member. At the same time you have to maintain a continuous membership in the National Association of Social Workers, the professional association.

If you hope to put that A.C.S.W. after your name, the accomplishment may seem a long way off right now. However, there's much to keep you occupied in the interim—tackling stimulating university courses, then the challenge of your first job.

Many colleges and universities offer undergraduate courses with social-welfare content. Illinois, Michigan, Wisconsin, Indiana, Missouri, University of California, San Diego State College, University of Georgia, Boise College, Catholic University of America in Washington D. C. and New York University are a few. An extensive, up-to-date list can be obtained from the Council on Social Work Education, 345 E. 46th Street, New York 10017, where you can also write for a directory of graduate professional schools of social work in Canada and the United States.

Your high-school counselor, Community Chest or United Fund office or other local social-service agencies may also have these lists.

If you have a college in mind, write for its current general catalog or request information about courses offered in social work, social services or social welfare—any one of these titles could be used to specify the department. You will find many social-service courses under the department of sociology or social science, or departments of anthropology, psychology or education. If not listed there, be sure to check for social-work courses under all social-science departments, including economics and public administration.

The requirements for a bachelor's degree in social service from Indiana University provide an example of the course of study you will be following. "Personality and Culture," "Recent U. S. History," "Elementary Sociological Statistics," "Public Administration," "Modern Social Welfare Organization" and "History of American Social Welfare" are a few of the course titles.

The University of Illinois' Jane Addams Graduate

Being a Professional

School of Social Work also offers an undergraduate
minor in social work. Here the courses are concerned
with the history and philosophy of social work and its
major methods of practice—casework, group work
and community organization—in both public and
private social agencies. According to the school, this
constitutes "a minimum preparation for those ex-
pecting to enter public-welfare work without further
formal education."

"In most colleges the objectives of social-service
curriculum for undergraduate students are similar,"
says Lester Glick, Ph.D., head of the Social Welfare
Department at Goshen (Indiana) College who is on
loan to Syracuse University, New York, to set up a
social-service program there. "The courses are designed so that students will gain insight into human
growth and behavior," Dr. Glick says. "Students
must also grasp the concept of social and economic
interdependencies, understand social-welfare philosophy—the values which are basic to social-welfare
activities—and the place of social work or social-
service positions in the total social-welfare picture.
In addition, students have to learn to communicate
fluently and acquire the ability to solve problems."

As you prepare for a career in social services, the
term "professional social worker" will appear often
in materials you read and will be used frequently by
practitioners or counselors with whom you discuss

37

your plans. In social work, being a "pro" means more than earning money for the services you provide, because you can get a job in social services without being on the professional level.

Defining the profession itself, Herbert H. Stroup, a widely quoted social-work educator, says: "It is the art of bringing various resources to bear on individual, group and community needs by the application of a scientific method of helping people to help themselves."

Many sciences are basic to the social-work profession: sociology, anthropology, philosophy, education, psychology, psychiatry, medicine, economics, political science, biology. However, the profession has its own structure and body of knowledge, which has evolved from these social sciences and is based on democratic ideals or values.

These democratic ideals may be familiar to you, because they are the foundation for many of our everyday affairs, but they will take on special meaning in social work. As you move along a career path in social services, you will have to decide if you are really committed to these democratic values:

A respect for the individual. You should be convinced that each and every person is worthy. That is, every man, woman and child has an inborn right to dignity and is entitled to his or her particular place in society.

Equal opportunity for all. You should believe that no matter what a person's race, religion or creed, politics or economic status, he should be able to develop according to his abilities and capacities for learning.

A belief that individuals have the right to decide what their needs are and how these needs should be met. In other words, a person should be able to work out his own way for improving his life, using self-help methods rather than having things done for and to him.

A sense of responsibility toward society as a whole. If a person is to grow and work toward his full potential, he cannot do this by infringing on the rights of others. He must recognize that he is part of a whole, that he lives within a framework called society which has laws and moral codes. And a democratic society or framework is necessary if there is to be personal freedom and individual development.

You are no doubt aware that it is one thing to have ideals and quite another to *live* them, to make them part of everyday existence and to help others put them into practice. To accomplish this within your own sphere of influence, you will need learned skills, formal training—in short, advanced education. And, as in many other fields, professional competence in social work requires more concentrated academic study than can be gained at the undergraduate level.

Also, graduate work provides the opportunity for a student to learn by doing—serve an apprenticeship, so to speak, or "gain agency laboratory experience." Nearly half the time in graduate school, which usually takes two academic years to complete, is spent in field-work instruction.

With an experienced social worker supervising, you will put into practice the theories, principles, methods, techniques that you have learned—work with people and participate in the helping process.

If you attend the professional school at the University of Chicago, you might do your field work in a comprehensive care center for unmarried mothers or with the neighborhood youth corps helping young people find employment. Many graduate students at Columbia's School of Social Work get lab experience with New York's Mobilization for Youth program. A University of Michigan student might work in Detroit helping a group with problems in relocation because of urban-renewal programs.

Because of the acute shortage of professional social workers all over the country, a few graduate schools are experimenting with accelerated programs that shorten the length of time (in calendar months, not in the number of hours of course work) required for a master's degree in social work. The University of Missouri School of Social Work in Kansas City; Syracuse University; University of Pittsburgh and

University of Michigan have twelve-month to six-teen-month continuous concentrated programs.

Other experiments and innovations are being made. In a few instances colleges are advancing and expanding undergraduate education so that students who earn bachelor's degrees are equipped for *specific* positions in social services. Graduates qualify as practitioners, but in a limited capacity. The more responsible, challenging positions still require a master's degree. And for some top jobs a doctor of social work degree is a necessary or preferred qualification.

Whatever your educational goals, there is no question that you should have as broad a background as you can possibly acquire for a career in social services. Just about everything you do can be related in some way to your chosen field. And the more you learn about yourself and your environment, the more you will understand others and their surroundings.

Meantime, though, there is the immediate business of getting into a college or university. It won't come as a surprise to you that college costs are higher than they have ever been. Magazine articles and newspaper stories on the subject abound. As costs continue to go up, there are some predictions that in the ten years from 1968 to 1978, the price tag on a college education will be marked 50 percent higher.

Unfortunately, there are no funds—scholarships

or loans—specifically earmarked for undergraduate students interested in social work. But that is no reason to be disheartened. There are many more resources to tap for financing a college education than have existed before, and these financial aids are open to all college students, depending on need and ability.

One of the first places to check is the college where you make your application. Financial assistance is also offered by state departments of education, fraternal and service clubs, labor unions, local industries, professional groups, religious and ethnic organizations, as well as the many Federal programs. You can get a complete list of government programs by writing the Division of Student Financial Aid, U. S. Office of Education, Washington D. C. 20202. The U. S. Department of Health, Education and Welfare also has several publications on financial assistance for college students, some available free, others for a nominal fee. Query the Department or consult your library or high-school counselor.

Your College Education—How to Pay for It by Sarah Splaver (Julian Messner, 1964) is just one of several books you can find in your public library offering guidance in college money matters. *How to Beat the High Cost of College* by Clair Cox (Random House, 1964) and *Planning and Paying Your Way to College* by C. R. Smith (Macmillan, 1967) are two others you might want to read.

And don't forget you may be able to get a part-time job to keep you solvent in college. Investigate the new Federal Work-Study Program. Also, *Changing Times* (The Kiplinger Magazine) has a report "Colleges with Jobs for Students," which lists jobs and pay rates available in over 250 colleges. Send seventy-five cents to Changing Times Reprint Service, 1729 H Street, N. W., Washington D. C. 20006.

When you begin to plan for graduate school of social work, the financial-aid picture changes considerably. In recent years more than 80 percent of all enrolled graduate students in schools of social work have received financial assistance. A document, "Social Work Fellowships and Scholarships in Canada and the United States," can be obtained for $1.50 from the National Commission for Social Work Careers, 2 Park Avenue, New York. The publication is revised periodically, and the 1968 edition includes a detailed description of sources of financial aid, including Federal departments and national voluntary agencies, and a listing of state and local agency funds available to all students.

Cathryn S. Guyler, director of NCSWC, notes that some "scholarships and fellowships, available through agencies, often require a work commitment after the period of study is completed. It is well to understand clearly the commitment expected in return for the financial aid offered," Mrs. Guyler advises.

Other sources for information on scholarships, fellowships and work-study plans are:

Personnel Services
National Jewish Welfare Board
145 E. 32nd Street
New York, New York 10016

Health and Welfare Scholarship Committee
United Presbyterian Church, U. S. A.
Board of National Missions
Room 1126
475 Riverside Drive
New York, New York 10027

National Conference of Catholic Charities
1346 Connecticut Avenue, N. W.
Washington, D. C. 10036

The National Council
Episcopal Church
Department of Christian Social Relations
Division of Health and Welfare Services
815 Second Avenue
New York, New York 10017

During graduate school, you will be creating what some experts in the field call a "professional self," along with learning the technical skills and knowledge of social work.

"I think one of the most difficult things for me to

master was this business of neutral emotions and impersonal relationships," says Mary Yoder, a student in the graduate program at the University of Michigan. "I had to learn not to be overly friendly—that is, become emotionally involved with a person who comes for help. By nature I'm an outgoing person, and I had to learn to keep my distance but at the same time establish a rapport or feeling of harmony. I found out my likes and dislikes and personal interests could not interfere in the relationship with my client."

Mary also notes that "all of this is necessary to create an atmosphere of confidence and trust so that as a social worker I can provide the best possible service to meet individual, group and community needs. There must be involvement, yet a backing off to get a clear perspective.

"In a way it's like developing a 'split personality', and that's a challenge in itself," she says. "But once I am able to combine both warm interest and objectivity in all my problem-solving sessions, I know I will be well on my way to becoming a true professional."

4

EARN WHILE YOU LEARN

Phyllis was from Maryland; Greg's home state was New York; and Janis was from Seattle, Washington. All three young people, just turned twenty, had joined VISTA to find out what social service or social work was all about and at the same time earn a small salary—fifty dollars a month plus living expenses.

Assigned to the Centro Cristiano de la Comunidad, Inc., in South Bend, Indiana, Phyllis, Greg and Janis worked with migrant families and were involved in just one type of experience open to young people who want to test their abilities and interest in social work before going on to professional school or deciding on a career in social services.

During her training for VISTA in Eugene, Oregon, Phyllis—who described her own background as "typically middle class"—admitted she was ready to give up almost before she got started. "I had to spend six days with a poverty-stricken mother and her two teen-age children, but one look at the filthy, barren rooms in the run-down house, and I felt like bolting," she said. "The stench was overpowering. They had indoor plumbing, but the toilet didn't flush."

VISTA had provided her with a cot so she did not have to sleep on a mattress infested with bedbugs. But the rats and mice raced across the floor at night, and it was so cold she wore extra socks, sweatshirts and slacks to keep warm. "I wondered how I was going to stick it out," she said. But she decided to stay because she reasoned: "When a house is cold and there are no clean clothes to change into, why should anyone want to clean up? A bath can be miserable."

She helped sew clothes for the sixteen-year-old girl, taught the mother how to prepare meals from government surplus food, sought needed medical and dental assistance, and spent long hours talking to the mother, guiding her in ways to improve the family's living conditions.

Janis and Greg had similar training experiences, and although homes where they stayed were clean, "the houses were ready to fall apart, and orange crates and boxes served as furniture."

Often, a "big trip of the week would be to the city

dump where they would rummage around for usable items," Greg said.

On their assignments in South Bend, all three VISTA volunteers agreed that, before living with the poor, it was easy to tell someone to pull himself up by his bootstraps, but they asked, "What if he has no boots?"

So they set out to help people find the "boots"— the resources needed for self-improvement. In some ways the duties of the volunteers in South Bend seemed tame compared to their initial training. They helped with remedial-reading programs; Phyllis taught soap painting as an enrichment activity in a day-care center; Greg organized a baseball team with migrant children. Yet the volunteers realized that many kinds of activities are necessary in rehabilitating the needy or helping people to live more productive lives.

Career testing can be undertaken also in a number of public welfare and voluntary agencies which hire junior and senior college students for the summer months. The job experiences give students the opportunity for an overall view of social work and agency services.

"Very few college students have an opportunity to work in a profession before they decide to enter it," said one junior. "I feel that the summer has given me the rare privilege of knowing just what I'm getting into in social work."

Another said, "The summer work experience meant a new awareness . . . but I cannot say that this process was easy or painless. Sometimes it was very painful—sometimes a sudden, startling thing, sometimes a physical nausea. I saw a lot of the pain and the power and the passion of life. But I learned through it all that I can adjust to the depressing, heartbreaking parts of this work. I gained a certainty I could not have reached any other way."

"Now I know—through experience not just through books—that people are capable of love, hate, hunger, pain and happiness no matter what their color, nationality, religion or background," a third student commented.

If you are interested in summer work during your college years, investigate the possibilities as soon as you can. Check with your state or county public-assistance departments or child-welfare programs. The Illinois Department of Public Aid has a summer trainee program, for example, in which residents of Illinois may enroll after two years of college. The salary in 1968 was $330 per month for two months employment.

"Students are hired to process applications for people seeking public assistance and serve as assistants in work with other agencies and groups such as juvenile courts and mental-health clinics," says Patricia Leonard, director of the Social Work Careers Program of the Metropolitan Chicago Welfare Council. "They also assist in agency studies."

While the Chicago metropolitan area probably has the greatest need for social workers, as compared to other parts of Illinois, Miss Leonard cautions students that "state agencies are faced with serious budget limitations" and it is not always possible to anticipate when agencies can increase their staffs.

Financial problems may plague other states' welfare departments, so, when you are ready to apply for summer work, it is a good idea to make inquiries about current conditions—unless, of course, you are able to volunteer your services without pay. Then you might be able to gain experience through programs of such organizations as the Mennonite Board of Missions and Charities, the American Friends Service Committee, migrant programs in some states or youth groups.

The Council on Social Work Education in cooperation with the National Commission for Social Work Careers (both of which are affiliated with the National Association of Social Workers) is actively encouraging summer jobs through communitywide projects called Careers in Social Work. The Chicago program just mentioned is one example. There are some twenty cities with centralized programs and offices, including New York, Philadelphia, Pittsburgh, Oakland and Sacramento, California, and Dallas, Texas.

In such coordinated community careers programs, a number of agencies—both public and private—

participate to offer a wide range of opportunities. To give you an idea of the types of summer jobs available, here is just a sampling from the office of Social Work Careers in Oregon:

—The Jewish Community Center in Portland requested four day-camp counselors.

—The Children's Farm Home in Corvallis had openings for three recreational workers who also served as reliefs for house parents.

—Two assistant vocational-rehabilitation social workers were needed for the Goodwill Industries.

—St. Mary's Home for Boys in Beaverton, Oregon, had places for two group workers.

—The Valley Migrant League in Woodburn needed a day-care staff assistant.

—The Bureau of Parks, Boy Scouts and Camp Fire Girls in Portland requested a total of 125–150 camp counselors and recreation leaders.

Across the country, in the Baltimore, Maryland, area, 104 students were employed in thirty-eight agencies during one summer. But only a handful of students could be placed in Dade County (Miami), Florida, social-service agencies.

You should bear in mind that many programs have more applicants for summer learning positions than there are jobs. The Summer Work Experience Program of Greater New York, for example, had 1,700 applicants recently and just 320 openings. Often preference is given to students who are residents of the area where coordinated projects are underway. However, almost all summer career programs in social work are expanding, and more and more agencies are cooperating, giving thousands of college people a social-service testing ground.

An unusual opportunity was provided recently for an Indianapolis student who had been a polio victim and could not use her arms. Not only did the girl adjust to an agency routine, but she was able to type by means of a stick in her mouth. Her presence in the Summer Work Careers Program proved to be of great value to herself, to the agency and to the other participants. She is now determined to go on to graduate school.

If you are accepted for employment in one of these "summer experiences," you will be paid from fifty to ninety dollars per week for an eight- to twelve-week period. Because assignments can be so varied, it is impossible to describe specifically what you might do on a job. Depending on the employing agency, you might assist with interviews, take a child to camp, assist adoption workers, escort patients to hospitals and clinics. You might be a group leader and set up a sports program or organize activities for senior citizens. In community agencies you might be assigned to help inspect housing, to find homes for the handicapped or to work on a survey of a neighborhood, listing recreational and cultural resources.

The Council on Social Work Education describes a

summer experience as a "be-in"—*not* just busy work
with a social-service agency. If your community does
not have a coordinated program that follows the
council's guidelines, maybe you could follow the example of a determined young woman, Jane C. "I
decided as a freshman in college to go into social
work," she says, "but I was confused by the many
fields of practice, and I had never really had contact
with people who have social problems. There was no
organized summer program in my small hometown,
so in my junior year I made up my mind to explore
this career on my own."

Jane literally pounded doors that summer, contacting each social-service agency in the area where she
lived. She finally found employment with a small
family-counseling service, and her first assignment
included home visits with a client. She helped a
divorcee with several very young children get a few
hours of privacy during the week. Since the woman
had no relatives or close friends, Jane could provide
the much-needed service of child care and offer some
adult companionship.

"Later on, after the agency gained more confidence
in me, I spent several hours a week in a motherless
home, helping a father and his four sons pull together in a unit once again," Jane said. "It was
extremely satisfying to know I could provide a much-
needed mother image for the younger boys. I was
able to create more family life by arranging for trips

to museums and simple picnics. We played card games, and I taught them how to prepare simple meals they could enjoy together."

In some parts of the country, summer work programs are relatively new or just getting started, so you may find many agencies have not worked out definite plans for use of student employees. Others may limit your involvement in the actual services because they are unwilling to turn over responsible duties to students. Or a professional staff can be so busy with their own duties that they have little time for student supervision. It would be a good idea to discuss these things frankly if you must track down your own summer experience in social work.

Whatever you decide to do in the summer months during your college years, be sure to investigate programs and opportunities near you. You might even be able to get an after-school job that will help you acquire intimate knowledge of what is involved in social work. That's what happened to Jane Falender when she was a student at the University of Chicago.

"An after-school job at the Orthogenic School for Emotionally Disturbed Children was probably what led to my choosing social work as a career," Mrs. Falender says. "My first task was play therapy with a disturbed boy who functioned in complete isolation. His development and eventual group participation, although limited, was so dramatic and satisfying that I had to find out why it happened. . . . Eventually I

got my master's degree from the School of Social
Service Administration at the University of Chicago,
and that led to my first job, which was with the
Indianapolis Children's Bureau.''

Although Mrs. Falender took time off from her
career to raise a family, she came back into the field
to become a ''second careerist.'' She is now director
of a Careers in Social Work program in Indianapolis
and holds an administrative position with the Community Service Council of Metropolitan Indianapolis.

If you do get the opportunity to ''earn while you
learn,'' remember that you are not only acquiring the
financial resources that will help you continue your
formal education but also giving your personal qualifications a trial run.

Maybe you will decide, contrary to Mrs. Falender
and Jane C., that you do not fit in the field of social
services. In that event, you have not lost anything,
because it is far better to make this decision before
investing too much time and effort in preparation.

It is certain, however, that a ''test job'' will ''dis-
pel any stereotypes you might have had as to what
kind of person goes into social work,'' says the U. S.
Department of Health, Education and Welfare, adding that more than likely you will be ''convinced
social work is the career for you.''

5

ON THE JOB

There are many similarities in casework staff positions within the Florence Crittenton Association," says Katherine Daly, field consultant for the largest organization in the United States for the care of unmarried mothers.

"The professional social workers or caseworkers with our forty-eight agencies about the country are part of a staff team made up of teachers, psychologists, psychiatrists, nurses and nutritionists. They usually have a caseload of anywhere from twenty to thirty clients," Miss Daly explains, adding that "FCAA homes are not mere shelters providing custodial care. They are treatment facilities designed to serve the medical, educational, social, psychological, spiritual and legal needs of the unmarried mother.

Thus the skills of many disciplines including the professional caseworker are needed.''

Casework is just one method of social-work practice, but it is basic to the profession because there is a focus on "cases"—that is, individuals or families who are trying to cope with social problems or personal relationships or both. And a professional social worker who has concentrated her study and practice in this area might take a job with almost any type of social-service agency serving a wide variety of clients.

However, in a Florence Crittenton home "most of the clients are teenagers," Miss Daly points out. "And one could be like Ann."

At sixteen, Ann was five months pregnant and came in desperation to an FCAA home after reading a newspaper article describing the place. She was the eldest in a large family and had most of the responsibility for the younger children, so had dropped out of school. Her father was an alcoholic and the mother mentally disturbed.

Ann had been dating a nineteen-year-old boy for over a year.

A caseworker obtained this information in an initial interview. She also learned that Ann had little means of support except for a job waiting tables. The money earned went toward the household expenses.

Once Ann was accepted in the home, the caseworker helped place the girl's mother in an institution and referred the father to an appropriate agency. The worker also counseled the young boy, alleged father of Ann's child, but because of many unfavorable factors did not encourage marriage. The caseworker did talk to Ann about her relationships with young men and marriage at some future time, however, and helped her see the value of returning to high school.

Despite this brief synopsis "it should be made clear that the caseworker provided on-going casework service to the unmarried mother in residence and assisted her in working out the most desirable future for herself and her child," Miss Daly emphasized. "This involved referral to a licensed adoption agency when adoption of the child was indicated as the best possible course of action, and helping the mother work through the emotional difficulties accompanying this."

It also included coordinating the various services within the maternity home and those of cooperating social agencies and medical resources, to provide help for the unmarried mother in terms of her particular needs. Miss Daly pointed out that the FCAA homes help young women from many backgrounds and walks of life—not all are financially destitute. A poignant story of a young ummarried mother from a middle-class family appeared in a March 1966 issue of *Together* magazine. Titled, "We Were Never Alone," the article describes the role of the FCAA agency and how it helps the parents of the client too.

If casework happens to be your forte, you will probably at some time consider working with the Veterans Administration. There are over seventy VA institutions located in every section of the country, and during any given month there can be as many as a hundred openings for social-work jobs. However, Delwin W. Anderson, director of Social-Work Service for the Veterans Administration, stressed that "professional training is required for these positions. Only after earning a master's degree is a social worker able to begin his professional career in one of our hospitals or clinics.

"Our caseworkers evaluate social factors pertinent to medical diagnosis and treatment, and determine what benefits are due the veteran," Mr. Anderson said. "A social worker collaborates with physicians and other members of the medical team to plan and carry through treatment. He or she would assist the veteran with posthospital adjustment in his own or a foster home or in a VA home. In addition, the worker cooperates with community social and health agencies, nursing homes, child and family services and public welfare organizations, especially as the services of these agencies are needed by the veteran and/or his dependents."

Mr. Anderson went on to note that "all social-work opportunities in the VA are in the career civil service. Persons seeking more information or employment should visit the Social Work Service of the nearest VA hospital or clinic," he advises.

Wherever you might practice as a caseworker, there will be many times when your recently acquired "split personality" will help you carry out your duties. For instance, you will have to be compassionate yet detached if you are going to help a VA patient get through the emotional impact of an amputation, disfigurement or paralysis.

In this and other settings it may take a good deal of creativity to help clients see they can benefit from services offered by an agency. With a few, you may have to admit failure or start over again. But acceptance of setbacks—and the fact that some problems may not be solved by techniques you thought would work—is part of your first years on the job.

A career in social services could follow a path that eventually leads to group work. Possibly you will start out in an agency where this is the primary method used to help people.

Gisela Konopka, a much-quoted expert on social group work, defines this process as "a method of social work which helps individuals to enhance their social functioning through purposeful group experiences and to cope more effectively with their personal, group or community problems." She also points out that one of the skills of social group work is "to develop a group climate which allows for the expression of genuine positive feelings while allowing also for working through of conflict, anxiety and other negatives. . . ."

As a group worker you would have to understand what forces are at work in a group and how group and individual behavior is affected by the economic, social, cultural and political factors in our society. You would encourage democratic action by helping groups develop leadership among members and resolve conflicts without "outside" intervention.

You would most likely be guiding organized groups if you take a job with one of the many agencies providing youth services such as the Girl Scouts, Camp Fire Girls, Girls' Clubs, Boy Scouts, Boys' Clubs, the Ys, B'nai B'rith Youth Organization, Catholic Youth Organization and neighborhood centers.

However, you might not work directly with youth in these agencies, but with adults who are volunteering their services to lead youth groups. You would be employed in an administrative or supervisory capacity.

With the YWCA, for example, "a person with training in group work would qualify as an associate or assistant to the director who is responsible for total organization of a community or campus YWCA," says Jane McAfee, personnel consultant at the national headquarters for the YWCA in New

York. "We look for young women who, in addition to having the educational requirements, show judgment and creativity in their work and are able to adapt, since Y programs take place in many settings, from the store-front ghetto building to a well-equipped new building in the suburbs."

It is possible to earn up to $21,500 per year as an executive director of a YWCA, but beginning professionals usually earn from $6,000 to $9,000 annually, Miss McAfee reports. She also notes that there is a "new dimension to YWCA programs as a result of cooperation with the Federal government." A few YWCAs sponsor Job Corps Training Centers for Women, and a good number of Ys are working with girls who have completed their training and are beginning to make their way into the business world. Counseling and the regular activities of the YWCA are among the services professional staff members provide for these girls.

With the Girl Scouts or Camp Fire Girls a district director or field adviser is involved in group work at camps and gives advice and staff assistance to volunteer leaders of girls' groups. Martha Futrell, a Girl Scout field adviser in southern Michigan, says one of the challenges of her job has been "learning when to intervene and when to pull back. Often the adult volunteers who are setting up Girl Scout programs in their communities want you to do the planning for them or to make the decisions. It's a temptation to do most of the initiating, but it is also very satisfying to see people grow together and accomplish on their own."

Similar group work goes on with the Boy Scouts, where there are some six-hundred openings each year for executives or administrators to coordinate community projects.

In the more than eighteen hundred YMCAs in the United States and Canada, youth or program directors have duties ranging from counseling individuals, supervising recreation and directing informal classes to guiding committees, training volunteer leaders and managing YMCA buildings. In fact, the jobs are so varied that Martha Anderson, who received her M.A. from Columbia University and now works with youth in a San Francisco branch YMCA, says, "Life is never dull! What could be more fun than getting to know high-school youth as they grow in understanding and acceptance of self and the world around them," she says. "They keep you on the growing edge."

The chief executive of the Flint, Michigan, YMCA would agree. John W. Davis says he works with people at many different levels of maturity, and that "there is a place for imagination and creativity in every task that is undertaken."

People of all ages are also served at Jewish community centers or YM-YWHAs, where the professional group worker is the "key staff member," according to Henry B. Stern, director of personnel services for the National Jewish Welfare Board in New York.

"There are 447 Jewish Community Centers about the country," Mr. Stern says, "and the social worker must provide leadership in activities ranging from public-affairs programs dealing with civil rights, to work with the elderly in 'Golden Age Clubs', to helping teen-agers discover their potentials in group experiences."

Although Jewish community centers or Ys are not under the auspices of a synagogue or temple, a group worker must have a Jewish background and an interest in Jewish life and learning, because one of the goals of the centers is to help members preserve a positive Jewish life within a democratic society.

In many agencies social workers use "group methods" right along with casework to help solve problems. Majorie Montelius, group services specialist of the Bureau of Family Service, U. S. Department of Health, Education and Welfare, says that "mental hospitals, correctional facilities for youth as well as for adults, family service agencies and residential institutions have all been moving from a wholly one-to-one approach to helping their clients in small groups."

For a look at how a social worker carries out the group-worker or group-leader role, take a few minutes to put yourself in the shoes of a county-welfare-department social worker in California we'll call Carolyn. Her experiences are a composite put together from reports made by some thirty social workers and supervisors in California's public-welfare departments.

With the guidance and cooperation of others on the agency staff, Carolyn initiated a mother's club, carefully selecting as possible members young women under thirty, who were raising their children without fathers and needed help to understand their youngsters' needs and problems, who were struggling to gain self-respect and overcome feelings of loneliness. All the women were receiving assistance through the ANC (Aid to Needy Children) program of California (the public-welfare aid which in other states is known as ADC (Aid to Dependent Children) or AFDC (Aid to Families with Dependent Children).

About twenty mothers were called or sent invitations to join the group for weekly meetings, and Carolyn explained how this experience might help them in home management and personal development.

The women were unanimous in their acceptance, so Carolyn made arrangements to have the first meeting in a neighborhood center, a building that seemed to be the most centrally located for all concerned. The meeting was to begin at 10 A.M.

At the scheduled time two women appeared, and Carolyn chatted informally with them to help them feel at ease while they waited. It was fifteen minutes before another woman arrived, and by 10:30 there were only five women in the group.

"It was extremely disappointing," Carolyn said, "but I could not let them know how I felt. The women were already restless and nervous, so I got things underway with some chatty facts about other mothers' clubs that had been able to find solutions to problems through group discussions. Then I asked each woman to introduce herself and tell a little about her background, education and work experience."

During the first few sessions, Carolyn had to face several frustrating aspects of group work in this type of situation. Individual fears and anxieties about meeting with strangers had to be overcome. Baby-sitting and transportation problems had to be dealt with. There had to be follow-up calls and individual consultations to get a larger number of women participating.

Some of the women were openly hostile. They felt threatened and could not trust anyone connected with the welfare department.

"I didn't dare become defensive," Carolyn said. "I knew I must encourage the group to explore their resentments and also to obtain more information about public-assistance programs so they would understand policies and regulations."

As rapport and mutual respect were established

and the women began to take a larger part, Carolyn indirectly guided beneficial discussions that attempted to answer such questions as: How can one parent be both mother and father for her children? How can an uneducated person get a job? How should one manage the welfare allotment? How should one deal with emotions and social relationships with men?

In many of the mothers' club meetings in California, women often admit they are unable to take any initiative because ANC makes them feel powerless to act on their own. But as a result of group sessions, they are learning to face this problem and to some extent overcome it. Community prejudice against ANC mothers is also a common topic of discussion. Many groups vent their anger and humiliation at adverse newspaper publicity, which often labels ANC mothers as "chiselers" or marks them as prostitutes.

Recreational and social activities frequently supplement the mothers' club meetings. There are recipe exchanges, hair-styling demonstrations, roller-skating parties, pot-lucks and bowling nights, plus other inexpensive outings that are valuable in this type of program. Women learn how to relate to each other in positive ways.

There is no doubt that, should you become a group social worker or use the group method in the social-service agency where you work, you will have to provide skilled leadership. But the role might be more analogous to the navigator on the ship than to the captain of the crew.

Leadership ability is also an important asset for anyone in community-organization work, the third method of social-work practice.

Mike Thompson is a professional social worker who has earned an M.S.W. with a major in community organization. Recently out of graduate school at Ohio State University, Mike's first job as associate director of a United Community Services staff took him to a small town in the Midwest.

In this position half of his time is spent in efforts for the annual United Fund Campaign; but he also has many responsibilities that would fall in the category of health and welfare council activities. Actually, Mike wears many hats.

Working with a citizens' committee, he helped them complete a study requested by the Public Housing Authority, then analyzed the reports they submitted and helped determine the need for a social worker in a housing development for low-income families.

Like many CO (Community Organization) workers, Mike is concerned that the community coordinate services if at all possible. He is, for example, guiding a study committee which is investigating day-care facilities. It will attempt to find out what kind and how many centers are in operation, how many families are being served and the socio-economic makeup of these families, and finally how many people need this service but cannot be accommodated.

In any of these projects Mike's role is never authoritarian. As he puts it: "I can't tell a committee what to do. I can identify problems, advise on priorities and give direction, but it's always up to the citizens' group to decide what they want and will do in the way of health and welfare services."

This may seem passive, but on the contrary, Mike has to be constantly on his toes. He has to help people work cooperatively and give them enthusiastic support when needed.

In addition, he speaks to community groups about UCS and the agencies for which it campaigns for funds. He assists the budget committee in its efforts to decide the best way to allocate money raised in the United Fund Campaign.

"I guess you'd be able to list dozens of roles a CO engages in," Mike says. "At one time or another I'm an administrator, planner, researcher, educator, promoter, salesman, catalyst, spokesman, broker, stimulator, negotiator, interpreter, analyst, coordinator, leader, enabler—and so it goes."

In short, he is a "generalist."

Being many things to many people sometimes has its disadvantages. "Things don't always move fast enough," Mike says, "because a CO has been trained to see the big picture and identify needs sometimes long before many citizens can recognize social problems. However," he adds, "I feel most successful when I see a previously negative or apathetic committee member or individual citizen take an action in regard to the community's well-being as a result of the influence I may have had, but acting all along on his or her own initiative."

And that is what professional social work is all about: helping people to become motivated from within to seek a better way of life and more harmonious relations with one another.

6
OPPORTUNITIES GALORE

You have just had a keyhole look at a few job opportunities for professional social workers, so it's time to swing the door wide open and see where else a career in social services might take you:

Join an Old Clinic at a New Beginning
We need MSW's—beginning through supervisory—who can contribute new ideas and flexible skills to help us:
Provide a complete spectrum of services to children within the community mental health center being built.
Expand our diversified program of community-based services. Professional staff of 12. Excellent personnel practices. Fairfield County living, convenient to New York City and New Haven. Salary $7000—$12,676.

POLICE SOCIAL WORKER. Aid the police department in developing and conducting juvenile control, community relations, and in-service training programs that include philosophy, policy, techniques and procedures. Identify, demonstrate and evaluate the use of acceptable social work concepts and techniques in a police setting as they relate to community, family and juvenile problems. Assist in development of interagency guidelines, act as liaison for the police department with social agencies, interpret programs to both disciplines and service the department as a consultant related to social change and community problems.

These ads were taken from a 1968 issue of *Personnel Information* published by the National Association of Social Workers. This forty- to fifty-page bulletin, which appears bimonthly, is packed with job opportunities. In almost every state there are hundreds of openings for career people in social services. To give you an idea of the variety of jobs, here are a few more ads, selected at random:

72

surroundings of the beautiful Northwest while working in a professional atmosphere. competitive Salaries—Merit System

SOCIAL WORKER for a 34-bed rehabilitation unit located in a 400-bed community general hospital on the Southwest Side of Chicago. The position also provides a challenging opportunity to work in an Information and Community Referral Center operated by the Social Services Department of the hospital. MSW required; experience preferred but not necessary . . . Starting salary range $8528—$9568, depending on experience and qualifications . . .

SOCIAL WORKERS. Established private residential school for delinquent and problem boys is expanding its program. Need direct service practitioners (individual and group counseling) and supervisors . . . MSW desired but not required for all positions . . .

SCHOOL SOCIAL WORKER. To work with team of 6 in large suburban school system . . . Case loads will be elementary school-age boys and girls . . . MSW or MS in education with social work major required . . . Beginning salary range $7200—$9330 . . .

ADOPTION WORKER. To complete home studies, place and supervise children in a large dioceasan-wide adoption department . . .

Nonsectarian, multiservice agency for the aged needs . . . CASEWORKERS. MSW required. Present salary range $7284—$12,048 . . .

RESEARCH SOCIAL WORKER. For a federally funded 3-year research/service program . . .

ADMINISTRATIVE SOCIAL WORKER. Reaching for an MSW to help plan and develop rapidly growing rehabilitation home for boys on 3000-acre ranch in western South Dakota. Salary $8500 . . .

Since at any given time in this country almost seven million people—blind and disabled men and women, dependent families with children, destitute old people—are being helped through public-welfare services, thousands of social workers are needed in the state and county welfare departments. A look at bulletins and announcements issued regularly by many of these departments will bring into focus the broad range of opportunities in tax-supported agencies.

There are always listings for public-assistance caseworkers, the title for beginning-level jobs in welfare departments. Regardless of where he is employed, a public-assistance caseworker usually carries a full case load, establishes eligibility and extent of need, explains laws, regulations and eligibility requirements to clients and other interested persons. Annual salaries could be anywhere from $5000 to over $8000, depending on the state and an employee's qualifications.

Public-assistance casework supervisors are also in demand. A position of this type "involves the immediate supervision and development of a group of caseworkers and usually requires training in a graduate school of social work and some social casework experience," says the Department of Health, Education and Welfare.

Other social-work positions in welfare departments would have titles such as child-welfare worker, child-welfare supervisor, public-welfare field representative, state director of child welfare, consultant on foster care and licensing, medical social-work consultant, director of welfare research and statistics, director of state (or county) welfare office.

If you would like a career in army social work, the opportunities are increasing. Men or women with master's degrees in social work may apply for a commission as a social worker in the Allied Science Branch of the Medical Corps. A social worker in the Army performs virtually the same tasks as does a civilian in the field, but his primary function is to help the soldier be an efficient, effective part of his military unit. Army social workers are members of the medical team and are placed in army hospitals, disciplinary facilities, combat organizations, schools and research centers.

At any of the five Army Surgeon's Offices in the country, you can consult with Army Medical Service counselors who will be able to give more details on social-service programs in this branch of the military. Counselors will also explain application procedures and outline requirements.

In a related field, "the American National Red

Cross has career opportunities in social services for men and women who want to work at military installations or other locations, helping members of the armed forces and their dependents solve problems they cannot handle alone," says Imogene Huffman of Personnel Services.

Also, the worldwide programs of the Red Cross, chartered by Congress, include the familiar emergency assistance at times of disaster, and safety and nursing services. While most of the duties in these programs are carried out by volunteers, on a national and local scale, the Red Cross reports that "it maintains a career staff that is responsible for the coordination and continuity of the programs as well as for certain specific services to the 3,400 local chapters." To find out about the broad social-service possibilities, you can write to: National Director, Personnel Services, National Headquarters, American Red Cross, Washington, D. C. 20006.

Some national offices of private (or voluntarily supported) social-service organizations have placement services or personnel referral services for qualified people who want to work in their member agencies. So when you begin to investigate possibilities for your first job you may be contacting such offices as the National Jewish Welfare Board, the National Presbyterian Health and Welfare Association, the American Foundation for the Blind, the National Council on Crime and Delinquency, the

Florence Crittenton Association of America, the Family Service Association of America, the United Community Funds and Councils of America and others which may help you with placement and/or advice.

There is a particular demand for men in some areas of social service. Travelers Aid Association, for example, wants male social workers to assist mobile and displaced persons where problems occur late at night or in remote places. Men often handle mobile units—vans converted to offices on wheels—which take services directly to such people as migrant families.

Male or female, there is a place for you in social services if you are qualified. In early 1968, New York State alone had "approximately 4,600 openings for social workers who had completed their professional education," said the executive director of the Social Work Recruiting Center of Greater New York.

Echoes of this type of comment come from all over the country:

From Massachusetts: "The job possibilities for the competent M.S.W. are practically unlimited throughout the state. There is a particular demand for people with a broad background who can set up and administer new programs."

In the Midwest, South and North, the demands are similar, and often, as in Oregon, you hear this comment: "Rural or less populous parts of the state are in dire need of qualified people. The majority of social workers seem to prefer employment in metropolitan areas."

One part of the country where there is a good deal of competition for jobs in social service is the Bay Area of California, which includes five counties: San Francisco, San Mateo, Marin, Contra Costa and Alameda. A recent survey of the health and welfare agencies, made by the Bay Area Social Planning Council, indicated that an M.S.W. or its equivalent is an essential requirement for most jobs. Even though many public and some private agencies across the country employ people with less training (usually a baccalaureate degree) to ease the manpower gap, this is not the case in the Bay Area.

"Many newcomers report working elsewhere in the United States, without graduate training, in types of employment that would definitely require an M.S.W. locally," reports Mrs. E. M. Reid, A.C.S.W., director of Social Work Careers Project in the Planning Council. "For those job seekers without professional status and without experience it is frequently difficult to locate employment in social work within the Metropolitan Bay Area." She points out that the reasons for this are high-income levels in the area; the many college graduates (there are more than thirty colleges and universities in the Bay Area) who provide a local supply of manpower; moderate climate and other advantages which "act as magnets" to people from other regions.

The emphasis on graduate education in social work is, of course, extremely important if agencies and institutions are to provide skilled services. However, there are some professional career opportunities that are open to people who do not have M.S.W.s but hold other graduate degrees and have developed comparable skills in related fields. Social workers in schools, or "visiting teachers," are examples. Their training has been primarily in education and guidance and classroom teaching. In some states attempts are being made to work out with schools of social welfare or social-work curriculum which would meet the requirements of both teaching and social work.

Many career jobs with the youth agencies do not require an M.S.W. But some advanced education and/or specialized training is specified as a minimum qualification for the responsible positions, which often have professional status.

In some instances there are undergraduate majors or special colleges for people interested in youth work. For example, there are three YMCA colleges: George Williams College, Downer's Grove, Illinois; Springfield College, Springfield, Massachusetts; Sir George Williams University, Montreal, Canada.

You might also consider the many opportunities for career recreation and park leaders. The National Recreation and Park Association, 1700 Pennsylvania Avenue, N. W., Washington, D. C. 20026 will send, at your request, material describing the various service careers, educational requirements and the colleges and universities that offer park and recreation curricula. The association will also help you with job placement.

All the possibilities for social-service careers have still not been covered, but later chapters will go into some of the more specialized settings. No matter where you practice or what type of social-service agency employs you, there will be many times when you will be part of a team that is providing assistance for individuals, families or a total community. Both tax-supported public-welfare agencies and the privately sponsored agencies work together. There is interdependent action.

This can be seen *within* individual agencies, too, as more and more people with various levels of training enter the "social welfare industry" to perform all the duties that must be done. There has to be a team approach. And even if you do not have professional status you can still be a vital part of that team. You can find out how, and in what capacity, when you read about careers for technicians.

7
A CAREER FOR TECHNICIANS

Are you eager to get into some phase of social service right out of high school? Or maybe you plan to go only as far as your baccalaureate degree and then find a job. There are several fields of social-work practice and many individual agencies which have taken steps to bring in assistants or "technical personnel."

However, you should be aware that this is done sometimes as a stopgap or emergency measure. Vacancies need to be filled quickly, and there is little thought about providing career opportunities.

Overall, though, agencies are trying to find new ways to meet social and economic needs through programs that depend less upon individualized services from professionals only and more upon the team approach that includes both professionals and assistants. This means that the career outlook for the social-work technician is good.

Assistant social worker, social-work assistant and case aide are other titles in use for those with less than an M.S.W. In army jargon, the non-M.S.W. is called a social-work specialist, says William T. Parker, assistant chief, Technical Liaison Office, Department of the Army. He also points out that the technician is an important link in the broad social-work team effort.

"There are no specific educational requirements for enlisted specialists," Parker says, "but they are selected only after a thorough and rigid screening process. Then they are given an in-service course that includes eight weeks in the classroom and eight weeks of on-the-job training."

Even though you may not enlist in the Army and in all probability will start your career in social service elsewhere, many aspects of the army specialist's job are also found in civilian life. One important responsibility is the preparation of the social history: assembling and organizing personal material about a client or patient who has been referred to the specialist by the social-work officer.

The Department of the Army notes that the specialist "must understand the importance of personal contacts with patients, possess skill in interviewing and be able to recognize the difference between relevant and irrelevant information. . . ."

A Career for Technicians

Whether in the Army or other settings, social-work technicians always work under the supervision of professionals. For example, as a Red Cross case aide you could begin your career in a military hospital and work with social workers, doctors, nurses, recreation workers, volunteers and others. You would help servicemen who are patients solve some of their personal problems, and assist them with family communications by writing letters or making phone calls. You would help patients plan for convalescent leave or for return to duty. If a patient is to be discharged from military service, you would help him apply for government benefits. And you would probably help train and supervise volunteers who provide some services for patients.

Casework assistants are also hired to work in "core units" of the Traveler's Aid Society. The casework assistant becomes a member of the team including two or three other assistants, a caseworker and a supervisor.

"In general, casework assistants handle the more external problems," says Laura Epstein, casework supervisor for the Chicago Traveler's Aid Society. "For example, a casework assistant handled Mr. J., eighty-eight, en route to his home in France after having visited relatives in the United States. Mr. J.'s train was delayed by a particularly shocking accident, as a result of which he became exhausted and mildly disoriented. He had ample funds, and his trip was valid and well planned. When the casework assis-

83

tant offered a one-night stay in a nursing home, Mr. J. accepted; the assistant then made all the arrangements. Medical approval was secured for Mr. J. to continue the following day. The casework assistant contacted Traveler's Aid in New York to assist Mr. J. from the train and to his ship. Train and ship personnel were also alerted to the elderly man's needs.''

In other instances, casework assistants are instrumental in providing Traveler's Aid services for desperate families enroute, for determining needs of clients during interviews and for follow-up work that might be initiated by a caseworker.

An increasing number of career jobs are opening up for assistants in mental hospitals and clinics, in after-care services for former mental patients, in homes and schools for the retarded and other institutions which deal with mental and emotional problems. The Office of Mental Retardation for the Department of Health, State of Connecticut, which has many model programs for the mentally retarded, recommends the use of aides in schools for the retarded and hiring people from disadvantaged neighborhoods who would be interested in preparing for public-service careers.

"While most of these aides are not necessarily hired as social-work assistants or technicians (in the strict sense of the title), they attend in-service training programs which will ultimately equip them for careers in a number of possible fields such as social group work and recreation," the department reports. "In one Connecticut city where aides are receiving such training, it is estimated that they will be qualified for professional-level employment within four to six years of the time they first entered the program."

Poverty programs in large cities are using a great many people with a high-school education or less from low-income backgrounds to work in community projects. Such aides work in their own neighborhoods and are able to interpret the community and its values to the professionals—and vice versa.

An aide who works in his own neighborhood can help the poor in many other ways: by providing information about social and recreational services; by being a model for people in the neighborhood to look up to; by assisting clients in such matters as filling out forms and getting to the public-welfare offices; and by being a sympathetic listener—one of the in-group, not an outsider.

In the recent book, *New Careers for the Poor,* Arthur Pearl and Frank Riessman describe an aide who has been highly effective. Some of his characteristics are important for anyone in this kind of social-service job. He . . . "is responsive in a low key, and is able to show some detachment. He always seems to be able to find and utilize the positive aspect of the situation, often in a highly constructive manner

. . . and he relates easily to the professional staff.''
The description concludes with the notation that the
aide is able to influence clients by sharing from his
own experiences, and does not tell them what to do.

There is a special place in social services for
women who have little or no high-school education
but would still like to have a meaningful career.
Visiting homemaker programs or homemaker services have been set up by some six-hundred public
and voluntary agencies in the country. These programs are needed in almost every community, but
they have been slow in developing. This is partly
because of the shortage of personnel to staff such a
service.

Are you wondering just what a visiting homemaker is and what she does?

That question might best be answered with a story
from the Children's Bureau, U. S. Department of
Health, Education and Welfare, which describes the
Valeno family and how a homemaker helped with
some of their problems.

The Valenos were constantly in conflict over the
upbringing of their five small children.

Mrs. Valeno, from a strict German family, tried
to enforce rigid discipline; noisy games, childish ar-
guments distressed and angered her. . . . Mr. Valeno, who was Cuban, tended to be far more easy
going and permissive. But to placate his wife, he
tried to keep the children quiet, just as he often gave

in to her many demands for unnecessary purchases they could not afford.

One day, after a series of family illnesses, Mrs. Valeno called her husband at work, shrieking that she was afraid she was going to kill the children. He hurried home and, at her request, drove her to the state mental hospital where she signed in voluntarily.

The next day, Mr. Valeno called the public child-welfare agency. Could the agency send a woman to his home to care for the children? The social worker could only suggest possible sources for a sitter or practical nurse or a maid since foster care was the agency's and community's only program at that time. Mr. Valeno resorted to maid service, but the children became more aggressive and destructive during the two months when she tried to care for them.

Soon after Mrs. Valeno left the mental hospital, against medical advice, the family again turned to the child-welfare agency for help. By now the children were completely out of hand, Mrs. Valeno was often hysterical, and Mr. Valeno was harassed and tense. This time the caseworker could offer several programs: day care, homemaker service and foster care.

After talking with the Valenos and the psychiatrist whom Mrs. Valeno had consulted, the agency agreed to provide homemaker service on a trial basis for one month. . . .

The homemaker set definite limits on the children's behavior. But she was calm and affectionate and allowed them the messy games that were recommended by the clinic as an outlet for their angry feelings. Quite soon, the children were responding to the homemaker's quiet control far better than they had to their mother's screaming and spanking. And Mrs. Valeno was less hysterical with someone in the home to relieve her of responsibilities. The tensions in the home lessened and the agency extended home-maker service, planning to keep it in force for perhaps a year.

Gradually, Mr. Valeno was able to accept the fact of his wife's mental illness and to see that he could help by standing firm against her unreasonable, excessive demands. And eventually, Mrs. Valeno's therapy helped her to see the relationship between her own very strict upbringing and her feelings of inadequacy and resentment toward her children.

No matter what your job at the assistant level of social work, you will be encouraged to continue your education with in-service training or at a college or university. This, of course, will help you improve your skills and advance on the pay scale.

As an aide or technician in the social-service field, you could not expect to earn as high a salary as professionally trained social workers. The starting salaries about the country are between $3000 and $6000. But as assistant jobs are better defined and in-service training programs are set up in more and more agencies, the salaries will improve. There may also be more opportunities for advancement to higher positions, although you will be limited in this regard since people with M.S.W.s and beyond handle the more responsible jobs.

Most states report that the public-welfare agencies hire the majority of the aides, technicians or assistants. Opportunities for such work are scarce in the private or voluntarily supported agencies. One of the reasons for this is that private agencies, with their higher pay scales, can successfully compete for the professionally educated people who perform almost all of their social-service tasks.

However, changes are being made. For example, the Welfare Council of Metropolitan Chicago has surveyed its voluntary agencies and predicts that "by 1970 there will be some kind of division of labor in Chicago's private agencies so that many more assistant positions will be available."

By contrast, in New York almost all social-service agencies now employ some personnel without a master's degree. Even though there are many problems in establishing work loads, responsibilities and supervision, the trend has been (and will continue to be) to add people of various educational backgrounds to social-service career staffs.

In almost all parts of the country, career jobs for technicians or assistants can be found with the Veterans Administration, juvenile courts, street-club and urban-renewal programs, community-action agencies, hospital social-service departments, housing projects, child-care institutions and programs for the aged.

If you want to work at the assistant or technician level, remember, that *you will be needed.* You may have to struggle through transitional periods and experimental efforts with the agency employing you, but your job as part of the social-work team can provide some of the same fulfillments and personal satisfactions that the professional receives.

8
ONE OF THE FAMILY

Says the Family Service Association of America, the national accrediting and standard-setting federation for three-hundred family-service agencies across the nation:

> Strong family life is our precious heritage. The family, more than any other human institution, shapes the personality and character of each of us . . . the ultimate survival of our society depends on the quality of families . . . [but] healthy family life can no longer be taken for granted. Because of the complexities and tensions of our accelerated industrial society, millions of families under stress need professional help in solving their personal and family problems. Family life is being battered from all sides . . .
> Family troubles and their by-products are tragic,

particularly as they harm thousands of children—
our future citizens—each year. There is a direct re-
lation between family stress and every costly community problem: family breakdown, mental illness,
emotional disturbance, delinquency, poverty, depen-
dency, school dropout and absenteeism.

Disturbed people cannot deal adequately with life.
A staggering volume of human failure and anguish
results in an equally staggering cost of uncounted
millions of dollars in care and cure.

If you want to do something to strengthen families, the family-service agency setting is a good place
to begin your career. Not only that, as a professional
you can expect to earn a salary in line with the
specialized services you provide.

According to Mary R. Baker, director of personnel
services at the association's headquarters in New
York, FSAA's recommendation for 1968 is a "minimum of $8,600 for a beginning caseworker without
experience to a maximum of $14,690 for the most
skilled caseworker with special staff responsibilities.
Recommendations were also made for salary ranges
on three different grades of management responsibility . . . related to size of staff, complexity of
program and multiplicity of management levels in
the agency. At the top grade, FSAA recommends a
salary range of $20,000 to $35,000," she states.

Nearly two million people are being served each
year in family-service agencies, yet the waiting lists
are growing. People with a wide variety of occupa-

tions and incomes—from the unskilled to the executive and professional—need help. They have problems ranging from incompetent home and income management to alcoholism and sexual deviation.

Each agency is basically a counseling service for marriage, child care and personal difficulties, but some agencies have additional programs. There might be special therapy sessions for alcoholics, or programs for families of mental patients.

"Or there could be foster care or adoptive services provided," says Robert Pollitt, director of the Family and Children's Center (an FSAA member) just outside South Bend, Indiana. "Most of the children we place for adoption are infants whose mothers are unmarried, and they represent all races and nationalities, as well as religious backgrounds," Mr. Pollitt says. "Adoption is a cooperative venture between prospective parents and the agency. Our caseworkers hold a number of interviews over a period of time with the parents, and the center provides adoptive families with specialized counseling as an on-going service when needed."

Some agencies—such as this one near South Bend —have residential homes for children. Some are affiliated with a Legal Aid Bureau or a Traveler's Aid Society or both. And the agencies go by a variety of titles: Family Counseling Service, Jewish Family Service, Catholic Family Service, Family Service Bureau, Family and Children's Center, etc. Usually an agency accredited by FSAA carries a notation, "Member, Family Service Association of America," to distinguish it from unaffiliated counseling services.

With the number of people age sixty-five and over expected to total 33 million by the year 2000, the need for constructive programs to help the aging is apparent. If you are employed by a family-service agency, you may be working with older people as they attempt to find their role in our society and seek self-fulfillment with dignity. Possibly you will be involved with programs which encourage employment for older persons in the community. Or you might work with projects that provide adequate housing, medical care and opportunities for leisure activities for the elderly. Or you may have a client who needs preretirement counseling.

Actually, the social worker's job in a family-service setting is best understood in the one-to-one or group counseling session. If you could follow a professional social worker through interviews, group meetings, telephone calls and other consultations as he or she works with a client or clients, you would soon know what family service is all about.

For obvious reasons, though, a worker could not let you look over his shoulder, so to speak. Nor could you review confidential case material. However, many disguised cases are printed and presented as general information. The essential aspects of real problems and situations are retained, but names, places and so forth are changed to protect the privacy of the actual persons involved.

With this criterion in mind, the stage can be set for the drama of the Kermit family, showing their problems and the social worker's part as counselor.

Here's the cast of characters:

Social Worker: Mr. Jones, A.C.S.W.

Father: William Kermit; age—fifty; occupation—foreman in shipping department of appliance manufacturer.

Mother: Alice Kermit; age—forty-five; occupation—clerk.

Children: Joan; age—twenty-four; Barbara; age—twenty-two; Sally; age—twenty-one; John; age—sixteen; Pat; age—twelve; Bill; age—ten.

The first scene takes place in the office of Mr. Jones, one of fourteen caseworkers in a family-service agency located in Chicago. Mr. Jones has received a phone call from another social worker at a speech-and-hearing clinic in the same city. One of the Kermit children, John, has been treated at the clinic for "stuttering," but the clinic social worker referred John and his family to family service because John's problem with speech is (in the opinion of the speech therapist) mild, but the boy is definitely displaying social maladjustment and anxiety. The Kermits have agreed to counseling, and Mr. Kermit has made an appointment for himself.

As the curtain goes up on the first scene, the interview is underway, and Mr. K. is explaining his son's problem to the social worker, Mr. Jones:

WILLIAM KERMIT. Well, Alice and I are concerned about John—it's this speech problem. It's not really stuttering they tell me, but he—John—has a hard time getting started when he talks . . . he makes faces, gets all tied up in knots. He has trouble expressing himself in school. He does better on written reports. And he is the only one in the family who has not made friends in the neighborhood. (We moved there a year ago.) He seems timid and easily embarrassed. The speech problem is especially noticeable when John is asked to repeat something he has just said. I think he just plain feels negative and that's his reaction—especially toward me. At least Alice—Mrs. K.—says this. She says I pick on John and put him in a position where he will fail, then yell at him for doing it. I don't think that's true. I want John to be an adequate person, and I don't set goals that are too high. It could be Alice is overly protective, although John is under pressure to achieve on account of his older sisters who all got A's.
SOCIAL WORKER. What kind of grades does John get?
WILLIAM KERMIT. Not bad. Not bad. B-plus average.
SOCIAL WORKER. Would you tell me about the rest of the family and how John gets along with them.
WILLIAM KERMIT. The kids all get along okay together and except for this thing with John there are no real problems. The youngest is a bit wild at times

—you know, boisterous—but all the family is pretty much outgoing. Sally and Barbara are going to college—just a year apart; and Joan, the oldest, is a nurse. She's the one thought we ought to take John to the clinic for help with his speech. All our kids still live at home, you know. They are all pretty close to my wife—much more than to me. . . .

The scene progresses with the social worker asking questions, listening, encouraging Mr. Kermit to give as much information as he possibly can about the family for the social study—the background on the family makeup. When the interview time is up, an appointment is arranged for Mr. and Mrs. Kermit to see the social worker together and dates for a family office interview and family home interview are scheduled.

Mr. Jones, the caseworker, must assess the family situation, give his initial impressions of the problems and decide on the disposition of the case—which is to accept it for further exploration. In copious notes in the case file, Mr. Jones writes in part:

John's problems appear related to the parent-child situation in the home. Apparently his being the first boy in the family made his birth very important to his parents, and Mr. K.'s feelings toward him seemed to have been different from those toward the girls. Some marital friction may have begun after John's birth and Mr. K. does seem to have some feeling of depreciated status. . . .

Mr. K. brought out the fact that John is very much like Mr. K. as a child, and this seems related to the pressure he is putting on the boy. Mr. K. admitted he had been a shy boy with difficulty in feeling at ease with people, but learned that this was not so bad once he'd gotten to know them. Mr. K. said maybe he expected more of John because a boy needs to be prepared to be independent and to know how to do things in the world. Mr. K. thinks perhaps he is impatient with John, although from his own point of view he is being reasonable. For example, he will tell John to do some simple task, and when the boy fumbles, Mr. K. will yell at him and tell him he is stupid, that it's a small thing and he should be able to do it. John just clams up when his father gets angry; then sometimes Mrs. K. steps in and reprimands Mr. K.

The youngest son, Bill, is just the opposite according to Mr. K., and Bill is easier to get along with. . . .

Mr. K. has been getting hard of hearing in the past few years and has to ask people to repeat things —especially John. . . .

The Kermits moved to their present location at the insistence of Mrs. K., and there was a period of conflict before Mr. K. agreed. Part of the reason Mrs. K. went to work was because of the high mortgage payments. . . .

With additional notes about family income and outgo, physical descriptions of all members of the family and details of the referral report on John from the speech-clinic social worker, Mr. Jones puts

98

down his impressions of the family interaction, which takes up several typewritten pages. There are also notes on the personal histories of Mr. and Mrs. Kermit, revealing Mrs. Kermit's feelings of martyrdom and Mr. Kermit's fears that his son will be like a brother who was committed to a mental institution when he was eighteen. In summary, Mr. Jones writes:

> One is impressed with how often the Kermits say ''we'' do this or that or ''we'' feel this way or that. There is little sense of individuality among the family members. None of the girls has dated. Another major aspect of this family is that the parents put much emphasis on high grades and on financial accomplishment. But there is tremendous confusion in the family's use of income and lines of responsibility. . . .
> In dealing with this family, one is forever trying to follow through on something, which soon flows into something else and leaves the worker feeling baffled, while the family seems to move with the tide —without there ever being any feeling of a beginning or an end to anything.

To treat this family, Mr. Jones decides to begin with them as a total unit since, he concludes, the problem with John is only one of several interrelationship difficulties. Mr. Jones hopes to help the family allow for individuality in its members—in thoughts and feelings—and to function as a unit for growth rather than constriction. He plans to see John only as a way to hold the total group in treatment and to help Mr. K. see John's problems as they fit in with the rest of the family functioning.

During a course of twenty interviews in a six-month period, Mr. Jones notes a great deal of resistance and "bogging down" on the part of family members. They cannot make decisions or plans, even about everyday family functions like who should wash dishes or walk the dog. They want Mr. Jones to decide things for them, but he refuses. Mr. Jones is often accused of favoring first one and then the other as he guides sessions; he is told he doesn't understand the older generation; then the younger generation charges that the social worker doesn't understand them.

And so it goes, with the family expressing pleasure that it could catch the social worker in its "web."

However, as the drama begins to near the final curtain, the social worker does not let the family "hold" or use him as they have been using each other. Rather, the family is able to loosen up somewhat. A lot of historical material about each member is brought out; attitudes are discussed; anxieties are expressed; some conflicts are recognized; roles and responsibilities are outlined. Mr. Kermit is not as concerned about John, and John is able to communicate fluently during the family discussions.

Finally, the family plans to have its own meetings

at home, and they decide to discontinue sessions with
the social worker.

In the last scene Mr. Jones writes his closing
summary:

Diagnostic speculation at the close of the social
study appears to have been accurate. Treatment was
used to do some individualization of family members, enhance reality testing and urge the family
toward mobilization and activity instead of stagna-
tion. The family currently seems to be in a state
of trying to find itself and a way to function. In particular parents feel kids are more "drawn out," they
have learned to treat them "more as adults," and
John seems to "have more incentive." Everyone
feels that Mr. K. has quit being so critical. Perhaps
Mr. K. summed it up best with his comment to the
social worker that "you haven't been able to get all
the way through the web, but you have reached us
somewhere down the line."

CURTAIN

9

ON THE MENTAL
HEALTH TEAM

B<small>Y</small> the time Nancy Outley became a social worker (A.C.S.W.) on the staff of a residential treatment center for delinquent and emotionally disturbed boys in Chicago, she had had to make many decisions about her personal life and her career choice.

"I didn't start out to be a social worker," Nancy says. "Teaching had been my idea of a career where I would be best suited. So I got my degree in education and taught sixth grade for two years. The students happened to be 'low-average'—test results put at least three fourths of them in this category—and they were considered to be 'impossible' because of their behavior problems. The school wanted nothing more to do with them—but something happened that first year."

On the Mental Health Team

Nancy reports that she was somehow able to "establish rapport with the kids, and we began to have a kind of group-therapy session as a part of each school day to work on such problems as temper tantrums, body cleanliness, hair care and relationships with others in the school. It was exhilarating, because the kids began to work out their own solutions and even helped each other. One girl in particular was helped by the group to see that her unkempt appearance and body odors were the basic reasons others rejected her."

From then on, Nancy explained, "when I had a good counseling day I felt more personal satisfaction than on other days when I was able to put across some of the basic academic subjects. I became convinced that social work was the profession for me."

After completing graduate school at the University of Pennsylvania, Nancy became the first woman to serve as a caseworker in the Chicago boys' home. One of her early clients was Mike, a boy of fifteen who had been repeatedly arrested for sexual deviations. Although he was severely disturbed, Mike was not ruled psychotic, and the court placed him in the home away from his widowed mother who referred to and treated him as mentally retarded. The mother had made this diagnosis after Mike had received a head injury in sixth grade.

"Mike was wide-eyed with fear at first," Nancy recalls, "and he actually did function as a retarded person. His mother had done everything for him, from writing his homework to taking him to school to all but tying his shoes. He was incredibly naïve and overprotected. But with support from myself, the nurse, psychiatrist, house parent and others on the staff, Mike slowly began to change from an I-can't person to a young man who could begin to make some decisions himself."

Nancy describes how ecstatic Mike was whenever he discovered that he could accomplish and achieve such chores as taking his turn at table setting in the dining room, or learning to read in school, or just reacting to other people in a healthy, productive way.

"After two years, Mike came to me one day, terribly excited because he had discovered he *liked* to talk to people. 'I even use my hands for gesturing— just like the others do,' he told me."

Mike was only one of Nancy's clients. "Others were angry, frightened youngsters—a few so badly damaged emotionally that they were beyond help," she says. "But at least 90 percent of the boys we worked with were acting out their fears and anxieties and anger in delinquent ways, and they could be helped to face reality and to learn constructive behavior patterns."

In the psychiatric setting, social workers do not always treat the mentally disturbed or the emotionally ill. Nancy recently made a job change and accepted a position with a center for retarded children. Now she sees adults and a few youngsters who are able to function at a mental level where they can understand relationships.

"My work is primarily helping parents of retarded children to see that they are not alone, or to help them get over guilt feelings—showing them they are not to blame for the retardation. Parents also need to share their problems and learn to treat their retarded child as much like others in the home as possible," she says.

Often a person in Nancy's position is referred to as a psychiatric social worker, and the term causes confusion about the function of such a professional as compared to a psychiatrist or a psychologist. Many people assume all three belong to a single profession. Even though they often work as a team, each has his own discipline.

A psychiatrist is a doctor of medicine who has specialized in the treatment of mental and emotional disorders.

A clinical psychologist has had graduate training in the modification of behavior, formulation of mental-health research projects and the administration of standardized psychological tests.

The psychiatric social worker has completed graduate work in which he has specialized in the evaluation of family interrelationships and the social background of emotional problems.

Social work in psychiatric settings—such as treatment centers, mental hospitals and clinics—has been in existence for most of this century, but the first workers in the field were called "agents." They were hired to help psychiatrists and were sent into the community to visit the families of patients and gather information for social histories.

Two World Wars, and the social services and counseling which veterans of those wars required, accentuated the value of social workers in the psychiatric setting. And, as has been mentioned, they now serve veterans and military personnel and their families in social-service programs of the Red Cross, Department of the Army and the Veterans Administration.

Widespread publicity and concern about juvenile delinquency and other problems of an emotional or mental nature in children also spurred psychiatric social-work efforts. The first experimental child-guidance clinics were established in 1922. At that time the three professions—psychiatry, psychology and psychiatric social work—joined in a team approach to deal with mental and emotional problems. This team relationship continued and became the basic structure for most other types of psychiatric clinics.

In an all-purpose mental-health clinic in New Jersey, William Nye, a psychiatric social worker, notes that "all three professions are represented on our staff. As part of the mental health team, I am involved in direct patient service to those whose problems are not so severe as to require hospitalization. Usually my treatment for children and adults is a combination of individual psychotherapy (the one-to-one casework technique) and group therapy. Work with children, for example, might include 'play therapy', where youngsters act out their problems because they are unable to verbalize them.''

Mr. Nye explains that "it is impossible to cover all the emotional problems we might encounter in the clinic. With children, some examples might be stealing, temper tantrums, nightmares and other sleep problems, or poor school work despite high ability level. With adults we might have to help them adjust to a death in the family; to overcome some excessive fear; to develop satisfactory personal relationships, such as getting along with fellow workers on the job.

"When a person seeks help from our clinic or is referred to us by other social-service agencies or professionals, the first appointment is usually an intake interview to determine what problems are involved and to explain the clinic procedure to the patient," Mr. Nye says. "Psychological tests may be given for further clarification of problems, and the person may be evaluated by a psychiatrist. Then we have a full staff discussion in which the findings from my 'intake' interview, the psychological tests and the psychiatric interview are presented. A decision can then be made regarding the handling of the case.

Later, I'll conduct another interview with the patient and recommend the type of treatment he can consider. If the patient agrees to go ahead with treatment, one or two sessions per week may be scheduled until the patient is discharged."

Community planning and educational activities might also be part of the clinical psychiatric social worker's job. This could involve meetings with civic groups and social agencies to design better mental-health programs for the community; leading parent study groups interested in normal childhood behavior; publicizing and presenting information on mental-health topics through radio and TV whenever the opportunity presented itself; and organizing research projects to determine the effectiveness of mental-health services offered in the community and whether or not all needs are being met.

"A psychiatric social worker might also provide consultative services for professional staff people in other social-service agencies who need guidance to handle some of their clients," says the head of a clinic in the Chicago area. "Ministers, teachers and others consult, too, on ways to counsel individuals and families and help them cope with their problems. This can eliminate the need for many persons to go to a mental-health clinic for treatment."

In a general hospital providing psychiatric services, the social worker functions in a very similar manner. He might see people from the community and also those on the staff, such as nurses, who are able to work but need professional help with their emotional problems. He also treats those patients who are hospitalized either for more serious emotional disturbances (but not so serious as to need concentrated psychiatric services) or organic problems that may be accompanied by emotional difficulties.

If employed by a hospital for the mentally ill or in a neuropsychiatric institute, a psychiatric social worker has, among other duties, the important task of helping a patient's relatives understand the nature of emotional and mental disturbances.

"Many people still look at the emotionally disturbed person as a disgrace or an embarrassment and do not recognize that he is suffering from an illness," says a social worker at a state hospital in Elgin, Illinois. "It is also part of my job to interpret the patient's family and social background to others on the professional team. Then, when the patient is able to return home, I must again prepare the family by explaining how they can help the patient after discharge. I also see people in the community who will be in contact with the patient—an employer, religious adviser, teacher and others—and encourage and instruct them on how to help the patient reenter the life of the community. Of course the patient receives couseling too during the time in the hospital and the transition period afterward."

Mental illness is a major health problem in the

United States today. "One person in every ten (a total of 20 million in the United States) has some form of mental or emotional illness, from mild to severe, that needs psychiatric treatment," according to the National Association for Mental Health. "There are more people in hospitals with mental illness than with all other diseases combined, including cancer and heart disease," the association reports. However, quick and proper treatment helps assure recovery.

This treatment includes new techniques and drugs, as well as the proximity of facilities—local clinics and neighborhood mental-health centers that allow the emotionally ill to stay in touch with the community, which is so helpful in some therapy. Moreover the expansion of psychiatric social work has helped relieve the overcrowded facilities for the mentally and emotionally disturbed.

There is still a long way to go in this field and social workers who have specialized in psychiatric training are in great demand in many kinds of agencies. Some have been mentioned. Others are:

—day-care centers

—sheltered workshops, places that employ the mentally and physically handicapped

—state mental-health centers

—rehabilitation centers such as the well-known Kenny Rehabilitation Institute in Minneapolis, Minnesota, where stroke, arthritic and accident victims and those with nervous and muscular disorders are treated

—halfway houses where patients who have been discharged from mental hospitals or paroled from penal institutions live until they are able to ease into the social milieu once again

—psychiatric units with the courts

—organizations that emphasize education and social action in regard to mental-health programs

The National Institute of Mental Health, which is a part of the U. S. Public Health Service, also employs psychiatric social workers, who are assigned to hospitals and clinics about the country. Some workers serve as consultants for regional mental-health programs or are involved in research at the Bethesda, Maryland, Clinical Center.

One of the main purposes of the National Institute of Mental Health, however, is administering funds. Grants for research, scholarship aid for graduate students in social work, money for building and experimental programs in mental health and mental illness are just a few of the ways the institute backs up and supports psychiatric social work and mental-health programs.

There is no doubt about the vital role the psychiatric social worker plays in the mental-health programs as he works with a staff that can be composed of psychiatrists, psychologists, nurses, sociologists, social caseworkers, community organization workers, case aides and others.

In the psychiatric setting—probably more than in any other area—the worker needs the support, knowledge and experience of other team members to reach the goal: restoring or maintaining emotional and mental stability for his clients.

Volunteering your services to supervise children or other groups in summer programs is one way to test your interest and abilities in social work.

Couples with marital difficulties receive counseling from professional caseworkers at Family Service agencies.

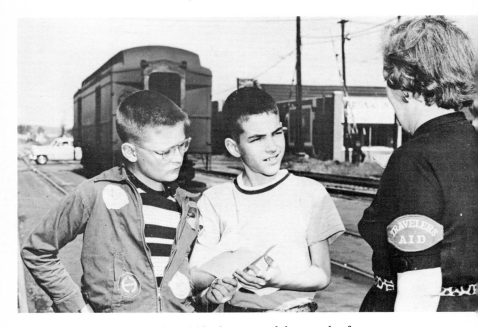

Each year Travelers Aid takes care of thousands of runaways, including a number of school dropouts. In many cases TA caseworkers work with the family at home to help solve the child's problems. *National Travelers Aid Association*

Staff Photo Courtesy: Clifton Guthrie, Virginia Pilot,
Norfolk, Va. & Norfolk Council on Alcoholism

Alcoholism is just one kind of problem a client may bring to a
caseworker in a social service agency.

Psychological testing and conferences involving parents, counselee and counselor are among the services provided by the Northern New Jersey B'nai B'rith Vocational Service.

Girl Scouts of America

Staff members of the Girl Scouts of America are involved in many projects in inner-city areas.

Joseph Jedd, Public Relations Department,
Girl Scouts of Chicago

There is a great demand for career people in recreation and park programs.

More than 2,000 full-time professional workers are employed by the some 750 Boys' Clubs in the United States, which promote the health, social, educational, vocational and character development of boys.

Mrs. Carol Stoneburner, Y-Teen director
of the YWCA of Summit, New Jersey and
Conference Executive, points out places
on the work camps' map to Y-Teens.

Keeping pace with the times, the YWCA
carries its program to the suburbs to serve
the people of rapidly-growing new towns.
Bureau of Communications, National Board,
YWCA

The president of the volunteer board of a local Urban League discusses an up-coming United Fund drive with the director of an Urban League in a midwestern town. The director is a professional social worker who helps in job placement, neighborhood improvement projects and other programs for the Negro.

Caseworkers, group workers, community organizers, program directors and other career people in social services work in neighborhood centers to combat juvenile delinquency, strengthen families and help individuals improve their way of life.

A social worker assists a recipient of Old Age Assistance to face the need to move into more satisfactory living quarters.

A social worker interviews a couple receiving Old Age Assistance.

A social worker for a department of public welfare visits a family to determine the financial assistance they will need.

A social worker pays a call on a poor rural family who will need financial assistance from the public welfare department.

High waters during a storm toppled this Atlantic coastal home.
Its owner and a Red Cross worker discuss Red Cross plans to help
the family in rebuilding.   *American Red Cross Photo by Earl Logan*

While recuperating at the U.S. Naval Hospital in Philadelphia, a
patient practices his typing with an assist from a Red Cross Hospital
Worker. Such staff workers supplement the work of Red Cross
volunteers in bringing welfare and recreation services to
men in military hospitals.   *American Red Cross Photo by Rudolph Vetter*

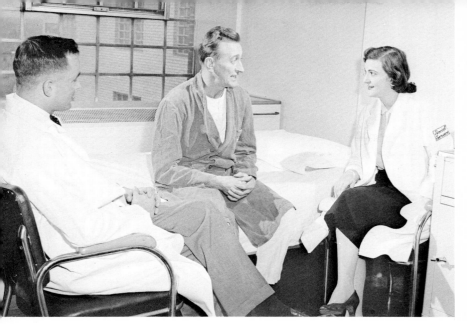

A social worker for the Veterans Administration and a physician talk with a patient in a V.A. hospital.

A doctor, nurses, an aide and a social worker discuss patients at a clinical staff conference in a Veterans Hospital.

An Army Social Work Officer discusses a problem with a worker in the field.

VISA volunteer Jack Long examines a successful graft on citrus stock, which was taught to the villager at the left by a local Guatemalan delegate with whom Jack works. Volunteers attempt to strengthen and encourage the work of government agencies in the villages.

Russ & Nita Rosene, A.F.S.C.

A young social worker representing Church World Service gives
technical assistance in a poultry cooperative in Epirus, Greece,
which has helped raise the standard of living of some 300 families.
Photo Courtesy Church World Service, New York

The Community Development Department of the Tanganyikan
Government, with aid from UNICEF and volunteers recruited by
American Friends Service Committee, sponsors home
demonstrations for women in Tanganyikan villages.
Audio-Visual Dept., A.F.S.C.

A probation officer is the link between the offender and
the community.

10

IN SESSION—SOCIAL
WORKERS IN COURT

Joe had been caught in a parking lot ransacking cars. He had a quota of stolen items to meet, as part of his initiation ceremony into a street gang. He is one of seven children, and the family is receiving aid from the welfare department. He appeared in juvenile court. . . .

Barbara is fifteen and is now a ward of the court. She and an older sister were taken into custody a month ago for prostitution. . . .

A mother in court is seeking custody of her two minor children. Her husband had obtained a divorce without giving her notice as required by law and had taken the children to another state. . . .

Hal is a truck driver facing court proceedings because he sold a load of valuable merchandise and pocketed the money to help support his two families. . . .

Allen is on probation. He was brought to juvenile court two months ago because he had "gone along" with a group of boys who had maliciously damaged sporting equipment and several small boats and trailers stored in a warehouse. . . .

The Johnsons are in court to file for personal bankruptcy as they are "hopelessly" in debt, having overextended their credit with payments of $350 due each month. Mrs. Johnson earns $280 per month. Mr. Johnson is unemployed and an alcoholic. . . .

Ellen Smith, age sixteen, and Phil Andrews, age seventeen, are in court with their parents to request a mandamus to be married. Ellen is pregnant. Phil has been in court before for auto theft, was sentenced and is on parole. . . .

These are just a few examples of the types of problems you may encounter if your career in social services takes you into the court setting or the field of corrections. You might not be hired by a court necessarily, although social caseworkers are often employed by juvenile courts and criminal (adult) courts. There is an increasing demand for social workers to handle domestic-relations cases, such as divorce and adoption proceedings, and it is not unusual for caseworkers to be "lent" to the court. That is, welfare departments and other agencies may assign a social worker to help clients who are involved in offenses against the laws or whose problems require court action.

Detention homes, training schools, correctional institutions of all kinds, including prisons and penitentiaries, need social workers.

"Because of advanced psychological information and sociological studies about human behavior, we know that rehabilitation can be a part of the correctional function," says the National Council on Crime and Delinquency, the professional council serving social-service career people in the corrections field as well as the public interest. "We also know that severe punishment and rigid controls are not the best methods to deal with persons who have violated the law. Thus social workers, skilled in counseling and therapeutic techniques, may be able to help inmates in correctional institutions to become responsible social beings, to find inner strength and to make constructive choices despite their imprisonment or detention."

Social workers are hired by state youth authorities —programs set up under state law to coordinate all rehabilitation work, education and medical facilities for juvenile delinquents. There programs have various labels, depending upon the state where they are established: Youth Conservation Commission, City Youth Board, Youth Service Board, State Youth Development Council, Youth Authority, etc. All of them attempt to *prevent* juvenile delinquency and to unite efforts in a state toward this goal by encouraging cooperation among courts, social service and civic agencies and institutions, by conducting research, offering consultation to youth serving agencies and helping to establish diagnostic and treatment centers.

The emphasis in recent years upon rehabilitation of the individual can be seen in probation and parole work. And there are many social-service career possibilities in this segment of the corrections field.

It is important to have some knowledge of what the terms probation and parole mean. Often they are thought to be synonyms. There are similarities, in that both use the same type of methods for guiding and controlling those who come under their supervision. And both probation and parole are committed to the professional approach in helping people to help themselves.

Yet there are differences.

Probation is both a sentence and a service.

The court has the authority to release a convicted offender without imprisonment by suspending his sentence. The released offender is still subject to court supervision, legally free only upon condition of good behavior. Such a delinquent (Juvenile) or criminal (adult) offender is placed under the care, supervision, guidance and authority of a court representative called a probation officer or probation counselor.

Probation laws and services vary according to the state or individual court, but usually a probation service is administered by a city, county or district court. However, a probation service can be set up in a separate agency such as a county probation department, or it can be a statewide agency or department. In New York, for example, probation is the responsibility of local government, and many county-welfare departments offer services to all courts, including city courts. There is also a State Department of Correction in New York with a Probation Division which oversees local services.

Most juvenile courts about the country administer their own probation services, or there is a statewide juvenile probation service. But some rural courts depend on services of county child-welfare workers if juvenile offenders are placed on probation.

Parole means release of a prisoner from a correctional or penal institution before his term has expired, subject to the supervision of a parole officer. When a parole board or other paroling authority has obtained a social and personal behavior history of a prisoner and has learned about the prisoner's attitude, present adjustment and potential, and then has determined that the individual can be paroled, a release is ordered with specific instructions as to the supervision, care, guidance and control of the parolee by a representative of the parole board, called a parole officer.

Parolees from Federal institutions are handled by officers in United States district courts. Adult parolees from state institutions are always under the supervision of representatives of state boards which grant the parole. For juveniles released from state "training schools," "industrial schools," or other correctional institutions of this type, there is usually a field staff to provide aftercare supervision. Or a child may be assigned to a family casework agency in his own community.

Those who engage in a career in parole or probation should be "persons of training, experience and devotion," says NCCD and stresses that "parole and probation workers are more than investigators. They are also counselors using the individualized personal approach in the study and treatment of offenders . . . through the process of supervision [they] assist probationers and parolees . . . to modify attitudes and conduct so as to become responsible, productive members of the community . . . they assist their clients to obtain employment and interview prospective employers for that purpose. Also, there must of course be concern for obedience to the law and the conditions of probation or parole. Those who violate the terms of their probation or parole in a substantial manner must be reported to the court or parole authority for rehearing and disposition. . . ."

The NCCD goes on to explain that "the authority of the probation or parole representative, which is ultimately derived from the court or paroling body, is generally used most constructively when it gives support, direction and encouragement to the efforts of the probationer or parolee to help himself rather than when it is used to implement punitive and coercive measures. . . ."

"Beyond these general functions there are specific tasks set up for probation and parole officers," says Walter Burker, a probation officer in Marin County, California. "These duties depend on the grade or level at which a person is employed—and this placement is often determined by civil-service examinations.

"In my particular county in California, the deputy probation officer—a beginning position for career people in this area of social services—has tasks that are quite typical of this field. The deputy probation officer has the responsibility of interviewing defendants and relatives, acquaintances, witnesses, complainants and others to determine the nature of the offense and whether court action is necessary. He formulates plans of probation and presents written or oral recommendations to the court concerning the disposition of offenders' matters," Mr. Burker says.

"Other duties of the D.P.O. include placing court wards or dependent children in suitable locations; giving assistance toward solving the emotional and social problems of juveniles under our jurisdiction; consulting and working with professionals in the field of religion, medicine and mental health and maintaining contacts with attorneys, district attorneys and various other legal representatives of the defendant and the state. Of course preparing and maintaining case records and reports are also important aspects of the job."

According to the NCCD, the opportunities for careers in the correctional field are more numerous for men than for women. This is due partly to the large number of male offenders, which far exceeds that of females in all age groups. Supervision of offenders is usually by the same sex. However, women are needed in the juvenile courts, in agencies providing service to delinquent children and their families and in correctional institutions for women and/or girls.

To get some idea of the variety of job openings in this field, all you have to do is glance at a job-announcement bulletin from NCCD. Listings in a recent bulletin included notices for "help wanted" from many parts of the country.

The California Youth Authority wanted caseworkers for reception-diagnostic centers or treatment units of rehabilitation facilities. In Delaware a casework position was open in a private correctional agency that provides individual treatment services. A parole officer was wanted for a Connecticut women's institution. The position involved working with women in the institution and on parole.

Caseworkers and group workers were wanted for a Minneapolis correctional agency, and positions were open in juvenile and adult probation, domestic relations work and family treatment units.

In Cincinnati, Ohio, a position as an assistant director for an expanding halfway house program was open, and the job included being responsible for fifteen to twenty adult parolees residing in a halfway house, developing a treatment program, making community contact on behalf of the parolees and conducting an outclient program.

In the correctional field—especially in probation and parole—it is not always necessary to have a master's degree in order to qualify for a position. But a college education with a major in social sciences is usually required. And completion of training programs would also be prerequisites for advancement to higher levels or to obtain or maintain some positions. Educational requirements are continually changing, however, and you can check these with college advisers and authorities in the correctional field. Civil-service announcements also list educational requisites.

For further information you can write to the National Council on Crime and Delinquency, 44 East 23rd Street, New York 10010.

One thing to remember about a social-service career in corrections is that being sentimental and overly sympathetic is of no more benefit to the person you are trying to help than being the tough, strong-arm type. You will have to strike the happy medium and bring both controlled empathy and surveillance to the job. It will be a challenge that will require a great deal from your "split personality." You will also have to be the type of person who does not shock easily. And you may have to accept more failures than in other fields of social service.

If you are mature, patient and firm, you have it made! You won't want an easy job and you will be compensated by seeing youth and adults brought back to a constructive way of life. And that is one of the most rewarding aspects of any social-service career.

11   GOOD NEIGHBOR POLICY

Community organization is a method used by social workers to help people mobilize to solve basic problems, sometimes in a particular neighborhood, often on a communitywide scale," says the National Commission for Social Work Careers. "The man or woman on the community organization job works with every kind of community group and its leaders —civic, political, social welfare, religious, business, union, neighborhood—as well as local, state and Federal government representatives; in short, everyone who has a stake in the improvement of the community. The groups involved in a particular task depend upon the problem to be solved."

There are many analyses being made of the effectiveness of community organization as a social-work method. As more insights and understanding are gained from the social sciences, it is possible that by the time you enter graduate school, the role of the social worker in CO will have changed radically. The fact is, the tempo of change in communities is increasing tremendously. It has been predicted that during the 1970's, changes in many of our areas of living will accelerate at a rate ten times greater than that of the 1950's. In other words, the changes that took ten years to bring about in communities of the 1950's will take only a year to accomplish in the 1970's.

Nevertheless, the here and now can provide some guidelines on what you can expect as a social worker in the community or neighborhood setting. Whether your graduate work is in CO or in one of the other social-work methods—casework or group work—jobs will be available in many Federally funded community projects. You could be employed in an urban-renewal project, for example, helping people relocate or rehabilitate homes and businesses. You might have a job with a housing program for the elderly or handicapped. Maybe you will help establish a comprehensive-care center, providing a variety of health and welfare services for a neighborhood in a big city. You might be working in a hospital helping those who are receiving Medicare assistance. Maybe you will work in a community-action program, a Job Corps center or a Mobilization for Youth program.

There is also a very good possibility that you might work in a neighborhood or settlement house in a large city. With approximately eight-hundred settlement and neighborhood houses or centers now in existence across the country, you will have a choice of location and type of center in which to work. In New York City alone, there are more than fifty settlement centers, thirty-five of which belong to a citywide federation called United Neighborhood Houses. Similar federations have been organized in twenty-two cities or regions, so that settlements can coordinate social action, speak for the people of an entire area, seek social reforms and unite to develop new programs.

Although some neighborhood houses or settlements concentrate on recreational activities or church-sponsored programs, the majority offer a wider range of social services than most other types of welfare agencies.

Whether in New York or any other major city, you could become involved in myriad activities in a settlement program. Settlement workers are called upon to counsel troubled families and individuals—casework services are always needed, with possible referrals to specialized agencies. Along with this, there are recreational and cultural services such as arts and crafts, family nights, dances, camping facilities, athletic programs and classes in music, dramatics, languages.

Some settlements have day-care centers for children of working mothers, plus dental, psychiatric and health clinics to serve the entire neighborhood. Other special services might include planned-parenthood clinics; classes in cooking and sewing; credit counseling; remedial-reading programs; legal aid; and sponsorship of housing cooperatives.

Settlement workers provide guidance for tenant associations in housing projects; leadership is provided for neighborhood programs dealing with such concerns as juvenile delinquency or issues like voter registration, new public schools, equal opportunity in housing and jobs for minority groups and other social and political reforms.

While no two settlement or neighborhood houses are alike, all have as their goals service in all aspects of life to people in the neighborhood and helping that neighborhood relate to the wider community. Other common characteristics are: the multiracial, -religious and -national backgrounds of the people, education in citizenship, and concern for the maintenance of family life and development of the individual. The settlement houses also serve as places for experiments in social-service programs that later may be adopted as regular governmental services or programs of voluntary groups.

The experimentation and flexibility of neighborhood centers allows for changes in services when needed. In recent years the relocation of families because of urban renewal has been a large part of settlement programs. So have efforts to help unemployed youth who have dropped out of school and the many nonwhites who are crowded into the core areas of large cities. Also, there is an increasing need for expanded services in the arts and creative activities so that settlements can branch out—reach all kinds of people who can work toward their potentials only if facilities and opportunities are available. Additional or new buildings are often a must.

Late in November 1967, a new uptown center of the Hull House Association in Chicago was dedicated, replacing the store-front offices that were used as a branch of the famous Hull House in that area.

"There is an intense need for social work in Uptown," says the center's director. "Residents in this section of Chicago are southern Appalachians, American Indians, Puerto Ricans, Mexican-Americans, Eskimos and Negroes, as well as families who have been in the neighborhood for several generations. The new building is one step toward bringing people together, breaking down some of the barriers that prevent harmonious relationships and helping people to make use of health and welfare services available."

When Adlai E. Stevenson III dedicated the building, he pointed out that there must be both public and private investment in this kind of social service. "In the long run, and in the broad sense, what is good for the ghetto is good for General Motors," Stevenson said. "Our society, public and private sector alike, is

127

in metropolitan America together, and if it goes
down the drain, or if it burns up, we will all have
failed and fallen with it.''

During the summer of 1967, R. Sargent Shriver,
then director of the Office of Economic Opportunity,
had similar remarks to make: ''Ignorance of our
fellow citizen's needs destroys more than it protects
. . . when a dog on Park Avenue eats better than a
human being a few blocks over on First Avenue . . .
when we are soft-hearted about sending slum kids to
summer camp, but then soft-headed about job-
training programs for their unemployed fathers.''

In many settlement areas, social caseworkers are
assigned to jobs that take them into the streets as
''roving leaders'' or street-club workers. Newspapers, television, movies have acquainted the public
with the kind of work this involves: meeting and
talking with hostile gangs, gaining the confidence
and respect of a street club or other aggressive group
of juveniles so that members can be persuaded to
stash the zip guns and switch blades and try to find
jobs, go back to school, put aside the violence in favor
of a constructive way of life. This is certainly not one
of the easiest kinds of social work. It takes months,
sometimes, to establish some kind of understanding
with a gang, to meet them on their ground and talk to
them in their language, while still maintaining and
representing one's own values. And just about the

only way to prove one has accomplished anything in
this kind of preventive work is to see the antisocial
behavior become less frequent.

In the community setting, agencies like the Salvation Army and Goodwill Industries provide social
services also. Goodwill is not usually considered a
"typical" social-service agency and often is thought
of as just an organization that collects discards. True,
Goodwill Industries, wherever they are established,
do use discards and salvage as "raw" materials in
their workshops, but basically they "rehabilitate
people, not things," as one director of a Goodwill
Rehabilitation Center put it. "A mentally or physically disabled person or someone who is culturally
disadvantaged can learn a variety of skills with
Goodwill and is put to work refurbishing used items
to sell in outlet stores."

Some of the larger agencies place people in training programs in which vocational-psychological testing and counseling is provided. Although supported
by voluntary funds, some Goodwill programs are
eligible for Federal-state grants which provide for
expansion of this type of service. This means more
people are needed to fill social-service counseling jobs
within the agency.

Some of the most lucrative positions in community-
organization work are with United Funds, Community Chests, United Community Services or Welfare

Councils. These positions may be with communities raising from several thousand dollars in a United Fund drive to cities raising almost $3 million. In an administrative capacity, the worker is expected to be involved in all phases of the United Fund program. In addition, some communities operate a United Community Services organization, as was described previously.

"Salaries available for these positions range from $8,000 to $20,000," says Charles G. Muller of the national office for United Community Funds and Councils of America.

"It should be understood," he cautions, "that a beginning social worker is usually hired as an assistant or associate only. Experience as well as graduate education are musts for most positions as executive directors of United Fund programs.

"Along this same line, there is a need for research directors in Community Welfare Councils and United Community Service agencies, with salary ranges from $7,000 to $17,500," says Mr. Muller. "These positions require advanced training in social research either in a school of social work or in sociology or a related social-science field. In some cases, practical experience in social research is also required."

Muller adds that "social-research directors are involved in the design of social-service projects and consultation to citizen study committees on sources of material and information needed for the proper functioning of the committee and, on many occasions, the actual collection and interpretation of necessary data for the committee. Research directors are also responsible for designing plans for evaluation of health and welfare programs and in this capacity function with Community Welfare Councils, United Funds and member agencies as technical consultants."

In any kind of CO work, you will have contact or involvement with a broad spectrum of social-service agencies—as varied as the color wheel itself. For example, there are 127 United Appeal member agencies in the Greater Cincinnati area. To show the range of health and welfare activities, here are a few of them:

Adult Deaf Welfare Society
Air Pollution Control League
Arthritis Foundation
Better Housing League
Booth Memorial Hospital
Boys' Clubs of Cincinnati
Boy Scouts of America, Dan Beard Council
Camp Fire Girls, Cincinnati Council
Cancer Control Council
Catholic Charities of the Archdiocese of Cincinnati
Catholic Social Service Bureau

Central Psychiatric Clinic
Child Guidance Home
Christ Child Day Nursery
Cincinnati Association for the Blind
Cincinnati Speech and Hearing Center
Council of Churches of Greater Cincinnati, Social
    Service Department
Diabetes Association
Family Service of the Cincinnati Area
Findlay Street Neighborhood House
Glen Manor—Home for the Jewish Aged
Greater Cincinnati Council for Epilepsy
Greater Cincinnati Federation of Settlements and
    Neighborhood Centers
Hamilton County Big Brothers Association
Hamilton County Diagnostic Clinic for the Mentally
    Retarded
Holly Hill Protestant Children's Home
Home Aid Service
Home for Aged Colored Women
Jewish Community Center
Jewish Family Service Bureau
Legal Aid Society
Mental Health Association
New Orphan Asylum for Children
Ohio Valley Goodwill Industries Rehabilitation
    Center
Red Cross, Cincinnati Area Chapter
St. Joseph Infant and Maternity Home

Salvation Army, Cincinnati
School of Social Work, Cincinnati
Traveler's Aid Society of Cincinnati, Inc.
United Cerebral Palsy of Cincinnati
Urban League of Greater Cincinnati
United Service Organizations (USO)
Visiting Nurse Association
Young Men's Christian Association of Cincinnati
and Hamilton County
Young Women's Christian Association, Cincinnati

Added to this partial list are public-welfare agencies and private agencies which are not members of the United Appeal.

"No matter where you work in CO, you should know as much about all the sources for health and welfare services as you possibly can," advises William MacDonough, who has directed several United Fund programs and community centers in Massachusetts, Connecticut, Ohio, Michigan and Indiana. "Whether in a small town, large city or metropolitan area, there is a trend in social welfare toward coordination of public and private social services. For many years the agencies supported by voluntary contributions were in charge of community organization and social planning. Government programs were set up along rigid lines with no attempt to develop citizen participation or interagency services. However, this is changing dramatically and rapidly. It appears that in the near future there will be much more inter-weaving of public and private social services and much more interdependency. This should cut down on duplication of services and result in more and better community programs to serve the needs of a larger number of citizens."

To keep up to date on what is going on in CO and the career possibilities in this field, there are several places where you can obtain further information. Write to:

Council of Jewish Federations and Welfare Funds
729 Seventh Avenue
New York, N. Y. 10019

National Board of the YWCA of the USA
600 Lexington Avenue
New York, N. Y. 10022

National Council of Catholic Charities
1346 Connecticut Avenue, N. W.
Washington, D. C. 20036

National Council of the YMCAs of the USA
291 Broadway
New York, N. Y. 10007

National Federation of Settlements and Neighbor-hood Centers
232 Madison Avenue
New York, N. Y. 10016

National Urban League
14 E. 48th Street
New York, N. Y. 10017

United Community Funds and Councils of America
345 E. 46th Street
New York, N. Y. 10017

Welfare Administration
U. S. Department of Health, Education and Welfare
Washington, D. C. 20201

Many of these agencies will tell you they have the social-work jobs "where the action is." But that is for you to decide.

At any rate, you will be looking for some kind of job *mobility* and advancement. You will want to move ahead in areas of responsibility and on the pay scale. The next chapter gives you a look at some "top jobs." You may plan to set your sights on one of them.

TOP JOBS

Maybe you can succeed in business without really trying, as a recent musical comedy suggested, but in social-service careers this hardly applies. The top jobs—in status and salary—are open only to those with the required experience and education.

Social-work research positions, mentioned in the previous chapter, are examples. Along with United Fund agencies, there are other voluntary and governmental agencies where you might someday be qualified for a responsible job in research. The Family Service Association of America, with national headquarters in New York, maintains an extensive research department, collecting and releasing statistics and some theoretical findings on casework or family counseling and on problems of broad national concern such as overextended credit resulting in personal bankruptcies.

The Russell Sage Foundation, the Field Foundation, Rockefeller Brothers Fund, the Ford Foundation and Carnegie Corporation are only a few of the foundations which conduct research in and make grants to voluntary social-welfare projects. The Child Welfare League of America has a research staff engaged in studies of child care. The National Social Welfare Assembly studies problems of broad social policy affecting the needs of people; the Council on Social Work Education of the National Association of Social Workers does research about career choices in social work.

The National Council of Churches and other national organizations under religious auspices do research pertaining to church-related social services.

The U. S. Department of Health, Education and Welfare probably has the largest research staff in the social-service field. Through its Bureau of Family Services and the Children's Bureau, extensive surveys concerned with the *effectiveness* of social services are conducted, and certain social problems ranging from the dilemma of unwed mothers to child abuse are studied.

In the opinion of the Council of Social Work Education, any person engaged in social-work research should have "the social scientist's intellectual curiosity and familiarity with techniques of gathering and evaluating data. In addition, he should have knowledge of basic social-work practice and experience in working with social agencies, for he must be able to visualize the human beings behind his statistical data. He should know enough about what is going on in all the fields of social work to be able to distinguish between important and insignificant areas for investigation."

The council points out that all students during their professional preparation become familiar with research and acquire some skills in survey techniques. But a research specialist needs more than this brief exposure or familiarity with methods. Doctoral study is considered the best preparation for a career in social-work research.

A D.S.W. or Ph.D. is also a preferred requirement for faculty members on a staff in a graduate school of social work. This "top job" could involve field instruction or classroom teaching or both. Before attempting to teach the theories and methods of social work and social services to others, many people in teaching positions have had some experience as social-work practitioners in addition to their academic training.

Administrators or executives in social-service careers are not numerous, but these positions, too, are top jobs that bring above-average salaries. Usually these positions involve more than supervision of caseworkers or others on a staff. An administrator might supervise an agency's expansion program, organize jobs and duties so that there is maximum efficiency, economize where possible, upgrade standards and actual services if needed, execute policies of a governing board.

Mrs. Carolyn Selling, A.C.S.W., director of a social-work careers office in Portland, Oregon, is in an administrative position which is, as she puts it, "deeply involved in helping alleviate the increasingly critical manpower situation in the field of social welfare. I feel keenly my responsibility to put forth every effort to see to it that people who need help are able to get it," she says. Recruiting future social workers through programs sponsored by the careers office is one means to that end.

"The satisfactions in this type of work are different from—but no less than—those of casework, the first thought of most people who want to do social work," Mrs. Selling points out. "Although the frustrations are here, just as they are in other settings—in terms of being unable to do as much as we know needs to be done—the pros far outweigh the cons, and I would not trade this work for anything."

In describing how she eventually worked into this job, Mrs. Selling explains that she "got hooked on social work at a very early age" when members of her family were putting into action their concern for the tremendous numbers of refugees coming into Portland at that time. "I certainly had no appreciation for the traumatic nature of the experiences of these immigrants, or any awareness of the desperate need they had for what we now know as 'intensive casework'," she says. "At any rate, I began to look more closely at my own community and to see many other groups who were not getting what I felt was a fair allotment of life's goodies."

After attaining a baccalaureate degree in social welfare, "I started as a caseworker for the State Public Welfare Commission," Mrs. Selling says. "But it did not take me long to recognize that the clients I was seeing—mostly people on old-age assistance—needed a great deal more than I, a green kid of twenty-one, could give them. I enjoyed visiting them, but felt terribly frustrated in what I could do for them. That was when the idea of graduate school hit me. Just as I was applying for admittance, my fiancé came home from the European Theater of Operations [World War II], and I elected to get my M.R.S. rather than my M.S.W. So it was eighteen years and three children later, when a graduate school of social work opened its doors in Portland, that I entered the first class admitted. I felt then as I do now: Social work is far and away the best of all professions!"

Another administrator in a top job says that her position came about because she "combined an ability in writing and an undergraduate degree in English with my experience as a caseworker plus a master's

140

degree in social work." Alice S. Adler, assistant director for public relations at the Family Service Association of America, points out that she has used this combination to "become a kind of interpreter within the field of social work." She adds that social work "is indeed a field that is replete with opportunities for the career woman."

Of course, the male executive cannot be overlooked. The top-paying, prestige jobs to which men often aspire are most commonly found in administration, or in teaching and research. In fact, a recent survey by NASW shows that of the nearly four-thousand 1967 graduates of schools of social work, "men . . . assumed positions in administration and community organization, the ratio between male and female graduates being almost four to one and more than two to one respectively." The study also concludes that "by far the largest single group by type of practice and sex were female caseworkers. They constituted 47.2 percent of the 1967 graduates and outnumbered male caseworkers almost two to one."

However, it should not be assumed that practitioners are unable to get top jobs. The caseworker can also advance.

Mrs. Virginia Nortdurf, who has been a caseworker in many settings including the corrections field, schools and family counseling, has a position now as chief psychiatric social worker in an adult- and child-guidance clinic. She carries a full caseload

CAREERS IN SOCIAL SERVICE

and also oversees all intake screening, is part of the diagnostic team which includes caseworkers, psychologists and psychiatrists, is the liaison between the clinic and other social agencies in the community and helps set up interagency agreements so services will not be duplicated, and helps direct follow-up programs for severely disturbed patients who need hospitalization.

As an A.C.S.W., Mrs. Nortdurf supervises and trains beginning social workers, and especially enjoys the challenge of orienting her staff to the group-work method. Highly respected in the community, she sums up her job in this way:

"There is no doubt that there is a great deal of pressure in this kind of work—no matter what the level of responsibility. Day after day we see people with fears, anxieties and tensions. They come to the clinic because they 'hurt', but this hurt can not be defined or localized. Yet the challenge to help these patients is what keeps me coming to my job eagerly. That plus the diversity.

"No two people are alike," Mrs. Nortdurf says, "and even though they may have common problems, none can be treated in the exact same way. And the satisfaction of being able to help a child become more outgoing and pick up in school performance after coming to us withdrawn, antisocial and with no interest in his studies is just one kind of reward. Or maybe a young wife has just lost her husband, and we have

142

to help her grieve—that is, encourage her to release her emotions and not be afraid to let others see how she feels. It's rough. It's demanding. It's exhausting. But I wouldn't trade this job for any other."

Akin to the clinic counselor is the social worker in private practice, whose income and status in the community may be above average. As with any other professional in private practice, his salary would vary according to need for the particular service offered and his acceptance by the public.

Private social-work practice claims a relatively small number of practitioners, and many professionals oppose "private" practice on the grounds that this takes it out of the realm of what professional social work really is: serving socially and economically disadvantaged individuals in a community on a nonprofit basis through tax-supported or voluntary organizations. But those who favor private social-work practice say this is necessary in order to reach the total community—even those who are self-supporting—and does not violate any definition or set of values and beliefs of social work.

Although private practice is a controversial issue, there are national standards set up by NASW. Anyone in private practice should be a member of the Academy of Certified Social Workers, and have "five years of acceptable full-time experience in agencies providing supervision by professionally trained social workers, of which two years were in one agency consecutively under such supervision, while giving direct service and using the method or methods to be used in private practice.''

Wherever your career in social services takes you, you will be able to advance far more rapidly than in most other professions. As a professional your skills, techniques and experience will be applicable in almost all types of social-service agencies. Not only is it possible to move from one type of agency to another (such as from a public-welfare department to a neighborhood center to a family-service agency and so on), but it is also possible to select where you would like to work—that is, the geographical location.

Because you will not be limited to one particular setting or field of social work, you will be able to take advantage of positions of increasing responsibility almost anywhere there are vacancies.

Yet you will also have to keep continually abreast of what is going on in social welfare and social work. This means attending state and regional conferences on social work, reading abstracts and journals concerned with social welfare and keeping well informed on national and local events—legislation, government activities, economics and so forth. So many things can affect the social welfare of a community and your role as a leader in the field.

13

FOREIGN SERVICE

Are you part of the "restless generation," as today's activists are being dubbed? Do you want to travel abroad? Are you looking for a way to have a "working holiday"—in the sense that adventure and new experiences go along with hard labor? In short, do you want to begin your career by taking a social-service job overseas?

The expanding role of social work and the demand for more and more social-welfare personnel is not limited by any means to the United States—or even to the North American continent. An international survey by the Department of Economic and Social Affairs of the United Nations notes that "nations at every stage of development in every region of the world . . . embracing every social philosophy and political system . . . need trained and experienced personnel" in social work, and that wider opportunities for service are emerging continually.

While each country or region of the world has its own social-welfare policies and for the most part hires indigenous personnel, thousands of Americans and Europeans can and do find opportunities in foreign countries.

Often these opportunities are with international or national voluntary service organizations which have programs in many developing areas of the world. The Protestant World Council of Churches, the International Council of Catholic Charities and the Jewish vocational-training programs of the international Organization for Rehabilitation through Training are a few international social welfare organizations with world-wide religious affiliations. Personnel of these organizations work, in many instances, with or through programs sponsored by the United Nations.

The UN itself "does not employ social workers strictly in their professional capacities," says Jean Iliovici, chief of Social Welfare Services Section of the UN, "but rather as very high-level advisers to governments in the setting up of training programs, schools, social-welfare services and so forth."

However, establishing practical programs to bring the "good life" and social progress to as many peoples of the world as possible is specifically written into the UN Charter. UNICEF (the United Nation's children's fund) and its allocations to health and welfare projects for children about the world is one well-known program along this line.

There are other familiar worldwide social-welfare programs which have national, rather than international, sponsorship. Probably the widest publicity has been given to a U. S. government agency, the Peace Corps, established in 1961 to improve understanding between nations and, upon request, to help countries improve the social and economic conditions of their citizens. Accomplishments and efforts of the volunteers who have joined the corps have been highly praised by the press and officials of many countries.

If you are interested in the Peace Corps as a starting point for your career in social service, you will be able to find a wealth of material—books, pamphlets, magazines—on what is involved by checking your public library. Or write to the Peace Corps, Washington, D. C. 20525.

You should be forewarned, though, that the Peace Corps—or for that matter any social-service job in a developing country—is not for the weak. Nor is this an *easy* way to travel the globe. The work will require physical and emotional "toughness." And if selected as a volunteer, you will be required to serve the usual twenty-four-month term overseas. An assignment would place you in any one of fifty-seven countries that are currently requesting volunteers to help in development projects.

As a PCV, "you will be employed in the service of

an idea," as new recruits are told in introductory sessions. "The work of a volunteer is largely a matter of individual definition . . . you will make most of the decisions affecting your life and work overseas. While a country's, village's or family's goals may be clear, the methods of helping people toward their goals require imagination, patience and frequently a good deal of tolerance for frustration. To go beyond this will be at once your challenge and your opportunity."

The Peace Corps also reminds its volunteers that they should be "optimistic, adventurous, curious, persistent, determined, concerned men and women— people in whom the imperfections of this world inspire neither despair nor acceptance but a quiet, good-humored determination to make things better in the face of many barriers . . ."

The rewards may not always be tangible, but one of the most valuable returns is a new sensitivity or awareness gained by living and participating in a culture different from one's own.

Some of the jobs and assignments include: work in family-planning programs; developing community interest in child-care programs; work in rural cooperatives, on demonstration farms, in home economics; and teaching.

There are similar social-service positions available in Protestant, Catholic and Jewish agencies based in the United States but operating overseas. A few

Protestant groups have volunteer programs that were established many years before the Peace Corps and in some ways were patterns for the government agency, except that service in these programs may fulfill Selective Service requirements in lieu of bearing arms—although programs are *in no way* restricted to those who object to military service. No salaries are provided, but there is an allotment or maintenance paid to cover living expenses. For information on three of these write:

The American Friends Service Committee
160 N. 15th Street
Philadelphia, Pennsylvania

which is an agency of the Religious Society of Friends (Quakers) that carries on many programs on a nonsectarian basis;

The Brethren Service Commission
1415 Dundee Avenue
Elgin, Illinois

which is an agency of the Church of the Brethren that has two-year minimum-service assignments overseas for men and women;

The Mennonite Central Committee
Akron, Pennsylvania 17501

which coordinates overseas programs of the Mennonite Church, and sends single young men to serve as "Paxmen."

Pax is a Latin word meaning "peace" and this Mennonite program, although relatively small as compared to most United States overseas welfare activities, does provide an example of how this type of volunteer service operates.

At any given time there are usually over 140 Paxmen in service. In Vietnam, Paxmen give refugee assistance, distribute relief goods, teach, do construction and Agricultural work. In Haiti, the men are engaged in community development and agricultural projects and hospital maintenance at Grande Rivière du Nord and at Hospital Albert Schweitzer farther south. In Algeria, Paxmen are working in a multipronged community project south of Constantine, in a center where they provide vocational training for villagers and work on agricultural extension programs and contruction projects.

And so it goes. The openings and projects for Paxmen are varied—as are the lengths of assignments, which may be anywhere from two to three years. The Mennonite Central Committee invites inquiries, and applicants may request areas where they would like to serve, but several preferences should be listed.

Sometimes the problems, frustrations and strains for any overseas volunteer seem too much to bear.

This was reflected recently in a notation from a Paxman's journal:

"Here I am in this jungle where the scenery is the same day in and day out. Just brush, trees and my same old garden where I am trying to teach people to learn to like and grow vegetables. They think they can just throw the seeds on the ground and they will grow. They don't like to carry water to their gardens from the river. Anyhow, it is so much easier to just come into my garden and get a basket of vegetables free. Less work . . . there is no charge . . . I am no Christianized Santa Claus, though . . ."

Of course it is not always this bad, and once the Paxman had released his loneliness and frustration on paper he was back on the job.

When Moritz Thomsen, a one-time farmer from nothern California, joined the Peace Corps he, too, had to face disappointments and failure. Assigned to a Latin American country where he was to help villagers raise chickens, Moritz had to find a way to save the chickens first. They were dying of cholera.

It took many months of work and a great deal of patience to help villagers see what should be done about the disease. Many in ignorance and fear accused the PCV of killing off their birds. One man, Ramon, cried hysterically: "Before you came . . . I had nothing. But I was happy. I lived without worries. But now, my God, I am half crazy with worry . . . !"

Finally, though, Moritz was able to make Ramon and the other villagers understand, the sick chickens were taken out of flocks and more new chickens were purchased. And Ramon, who apologized to Moritz for the long doubts he had had about him, was ecstatic. He planned to eventually buy a hundred chickens which would provide him with a new source of income. "You know what I am going to buy when I am rich?" he said, beginning to laugh with delight at the idea. "A pair of shoes. Oh, my God. My God!"

In addition to the volunteers, there are many other social-service personnel involved in the various overseas programs of United States agencies. For example, the U. S. Department of Health, Education and Welfare maintains international offices. AID (Agency for International Development) provides technical advice and assistance for agricultural and vocational programs, reforestation, education, housing and other services in developing countries. The Veterans Administration serves an increasing number of veterans who are living abroad. The American National Red Cross has opportunities for overseas social-service work with armed-forces personnel and in disaster programs.

Church World Service, a department of the National Council of Churches which represents most Protestant Churches, has many social service and self-help projects overseas. Although Church World Service does not directly hire a large number of social workers, the agency does use social-service personnel provided by member denominations of NCC. And recently CWS has been relying on professional social workers as consultants.

One such worker is Dr. Charles Chakerian, A.C.S.W., chairman of the Department of Church and Community, McCormick Theological Seminary, Chicago, who was called in to review a long-term child-welfare program in Korea. Over a period of five years, Dr. Chakerian surveyed, studied, evaluated and reported on problems of abandoned children in Korea, children of mixed parentage, institutional care for Korean children and other problems of this nature. Then he advised CWS on how it could meet needs, how it could help in training programs for Korean social workers and how the agency could better work with other social-service agencies and governmental organizations in the country. He also made many additional recommendations on possible areas for developments in child welfare.

Catholic Relief Services, Lutheran World Relief and the American Jewish Joint Distribution Committee are other major agencies with religious affiliations using social-service career personnel abroad. There are many more, and space does not permit naming all of them, but the main thing to remember is that overseas work with such agencies does not necessarily belong in the category of "missionary" efforts. Instead, social-service programs today are putting increasing emphasis on serving the whole person—not just providing for his spiritual needs. However, you should bear in mind that accepting a position with a religiously sponsored overseas program usually presupposes a commitment to the particular faith or religion of which the agency is a part.

In all there are more than fifty American voluntary agencies that have overseas programs. Some do not provide direct aid for individuals, but staff members do work with governments or other agencies in the country where service is needed to help set up programs, establish pilot projects and provide educational materials.

If you decide to work abroad, you will probably at some time be asked point-blank: "Why?" The inquirer may reason that with the manpower shortages so great and with all the social-welfare needs in our own country still to be met, why should any social worker want to go overseas? Your answer, of course, is purely a personal matter, but you might agree with Pope Paul VI, whose encyclical letter of March 1967 outlined reasons for assisting developing countries. In essence the Pope said: "Development is the new name for Peace."

14
A WORD ABOUT
SOCIAL SERVICE AND RELIGION

It is impossible to separate social services and organized religion in this country. The two have gone hand-in-hand for centuries. All major faiths sponsor social-welfare programs and usually have established policies in this regard.

Dr. Chakerian, writing in the *Encyclopedia of Social Work,* says: "There is no general agreement as to what is meant by 'religious sponsorship' of social-welfare programs," but he noted that sectarian social services have certain elements in common—ties to a religious body, religious affiliation of a governing board, objectives and practices based on religious precepts. "None of these factors is static," Dr. Chakerian added. "Therefore the nature of religious sponsorship is always in a state of flux."

At one time religious bodies took care of their own—that is, provided social services for only those who were members of the particular Church. But this is not necessarily true today. Most religious groups now see social service as a much broader function.

Take the National Presbyterian Health and Welfare Association, the agency that coordinates social-welfare programs of the United Presbyterian Church, U. S. A. Mr. Alfred M. Rath, A.C.S.W., and an executive with the Church's Board of National Missions, explains that "programs of social concern have always been part of the church's fabric even though at times the motivation and expression may have been hidden under the cross-stitch of learned debates on the best methods of saving men's souls."

"A century ago," he adds, "the concern of the churches for social welfare was chiefly expressed through programs which had the highest potential for membership. Today the Church sees its mission in social-welfare programs as an expression of thanks to God for his concern and love . . . an integral part of the ministry of the Church, not an optional part of its program."

The types of agencies affiliated with NPH & WA cover the full range of social-welfare activities. For example, there are some fifty-eight community centers, nineteen hospitals, forty-nine homes for the aging and twelve child-care agencies, along with other community-service programs. And the organi-

156

zation has expressed a need for personnel at every level of social-work practice, including house-mothers, caseworkers, program directors, group workers, community organizers, workers in psychiatric settings and administrators.

The United Presbyterian Church also sponsors a program for graduate education in social work. Along with theological education at McCormick Theological Seminary in Chicago, students also may take courses of study leading to an M.S.W. that have been developed in collaboration with the School of Social Service Administration of the University of Chicago, the Jane Addams Graduate School of Social Work of the University of Illinois and the School of Social Work of Loyola University.

The Episcopal Church has also set forth its doctrines concerning social welfare. The Department of Health and Welfare Services of the National Council of the Episcopal Church says: "The social services of the Church combine a deep concern for human relations, the hallmark of all social work, with the added imperative of a spiritual ministry."

The department advises that the Church "offers a unique chance . . . to use your own particular skills and interests in a variety of jobs . . . [but] your decision to enter church social work should be made only after serious consideration of your own talents, goals and needs, and a careful study of the demands that will be made upon you."

Because there are ten Lutheran church groups in the United States, each with its own social-welfare policies, it is not possible to make a flat statement regarding the overall Lutheran approach to social services. However, the Welfare Division of the Lutheran Council in the U. S. A., formed in 1967, is working toward this end and seeks to define and co-ordinate efforts of at least four of the major Lutheran bodies. The largest of these, the Lutheran Church in America, sponsors nearly two-hundred health and welfare agencies and institutions and summer camps.

The Methodist Church, the Mennonites, Mormons, Baptists and many other Protestant groups have extensive social-welfare programs, agencies and institutions also, which have been established as "outreaches" of the denominations.

The National Conference of Catholic Charities is the official coordinating body of the social-service programs of the Roman Catholic Church in the United States.

"Traditionally Catholic Charities has had a major concern for children, older people, youth who are in danger of becoming delinquent and who are actually delinquent, all of these on an institutional basis," says Sister Maria Mercedes, S.S.N.D., Director of Information and Research for NCCC. "In the Family Counseling Division, or as it is frequently called, the Family and Children's Agency, there is the addi-

158

tional traditional work of marriage and family counseling, adoption work, care for unmarried mothers,
casework with delinquent and dependent children,
etc.''

Sister Maria points out that ''these services across
the country are conducted in 215 institutions for
dependent and neglected children, eighteen centers
for physically handicapped children, twenty-two
schools for the retarded child, eighty training centers
for teen-aged boys and girls, fifty-seven homes for
the unmarried mother, 357 homes for the aging, 280
bureaus, clinics and agencies for specialized social
services.

''In recent years Catholic Charities has become
more and more involved in community organization
in poverty-stricken areas,'' Sister Maria says, adding
that CO workers are especially in demand in Catholic
welfare programs.

However, she states frankly that it is difficult to
say where there is the greatest need for workers
because ''nobody has enough of them . . . job positions with Catholic Charities cover a great range of
activities, from the highly specialized and professional director and supervisors to case aides. Group
workers, community-organization workers and caseworkers are employed in the various agencies mentioned. In addition to those which require a master's
degree, often local offices accept students with a
college degree, especially if they have a sequence in

social welfare as part of their undergraduate preparation."

Additional information on Catholic Charities can be obtained from the National Conference of Catholic Charities, 1346 Connecticut Avenue, N. W., Suite 307, Washington, D. C. 20036, and from Catholic schools of social work—six in the United States and three in Canada—listed in the appendix.

Although Catholics have the largest sectarian representation in social-work education, this does not mean Catholic social services are "slanted," or that proselytizing is the foremost consideration. The virtue of charity is fundamental to Catholicism, but this is accompanied by professionalism in social services.

Basically Jewish welfare is not affiliated with any synagogue or under the direction of any religious body. Each field of service is autonomous. Therefore it would *not* come under the category of religiously sponsored social service. But there is a distinct "religiosity" in the long tradition of social service among Jews. Biblical and rabbinical references abound on the subject, and social action is basic to Jewish values. So is the concept of social justice and community responsibility.

This is brought out dramatically in a unique and recent publication distributed in Jewish communities and conceived during teen-age leadership training institutes conducted by the Midwest Section of the

National Jewish Welfare Board. Called *The Right to be Different,* the sophisticated paperback book edited by Elias Picheny, social worker–educator in Chicago, contains poetry, quotes and sketches of many Jewish and American leaders of other backgrounds "who sought a better world." Although this is not a book about Jewish social welfare in particular, it does contain "stories of American and Jewish leaders who were *different with a purpose,"* and made a contribution to our way of life, to society as a whole.

One of the poetic renditions may epitomize what social welfare under Jewish auspices is all about. For that matter, the poem could represent the creed of any dedicated social worker and humanitarian—the professional who has a "mission," if you will, not just a job:

LIFE AND DEATH*
So he died for his faith. That is fine,
    More than most of us do.
But, say, can you add to that line
    That he lived for it, too?
In his death he bore witness at last
    As a martyr to the truth.
Did his life do the same in the past,
    From the days of his youth?

* reprinted, by permission, from *The Right to be Different,* published by the Lionel Picheny Memorial Fund, 1961.

It is easy to die. Men have died
    For a wish or a whim—
From bravado or passion or pride,
    Was it harder for him?
But to live—every day to live out
    All the truth that he dreamt,
While his friends met his conduct with doubt
    And the world with contempt.
Was it thus that he plodded ahead,
    Never turning aside?
Then we'll talk of the life that he lived.
    Never mind how he died.

             —Ernest Crosby

If you seek a place in religiously oriented social work or social services under sectarian auspices, there will definitely be many opportunities. In some instances, you may have to accept lower wages than in other types of voluntary agencies, but the idea that a person should be content with meager material rewards because he is in "religious work" is not as prevalent as it used to be. The current trend in this area, too, is toward professional preparation, with salaries that are in line with the training.

You will probably not be questioned about your religious motivations, nor will you be required to join a particular religious group in order to obtain a job. However, you may be expected to have a commitment to the agency's goals, which may be based on religious precepts.

A Word About Social Service and Religion

In the past few years there has been much more "secularization" of church-related welfare agencies. Not that the religious foundations are negated, but rather there is more openness, cooperation with other faiths, an ecumenical approach and more emphasis on serving all kinds of people on the basis of need, regardless of race, economic status or religious conviction.

In the final analysis, a social worker may be motivated by religious convictions or humanitarian ideals or both. It is not the place here to argue the value of one over the other. This is something you may want to do on your own or in consultation with a religious adviser. In this field, as in any other, your career choice should be based on an honest appraisal of yourself and the kind of work for which you are best suited and qualified.

15
NO TIME FOR BOREDOM

The variety of experiences that a social worker fits into one day may seem unbelievable the first time you are exposed to a schedule. Very few workers have nine-to-five jobs. But seldom do you hear complaints about this. Nor do you hear much grumbling about the drain on emotions. It's all part of the profession—and the challenge.

Over and over again "challenge" is the word that seems to sum up so much of the appeal of social service. Mrs. Goldie L. Ivory, a supervisor in the social-service program of a Midwest public school system, refers often to the challenges of her job. And she is not just mouthing the phrase. Her eyes sparkle when she talks about her work, and her enthusiasm touches everyone in contact with her. She thrives on

the challenge, the demands, the jam-packed schedule.
A day with Mrs. Ivory can be exhausting, though.
If you want to be on-the-go when she is, you have to
pry you eyes open at 6 A.M. and be ready for a 6:30
meeting with school administrators and other personnel who will discuss a Federally funded (Title
III) project called IMAGE (Innovative Methods
Affecting Goals in Education). Although this is not a
typical meeting, there are many other situations
which warrant early appointments, and Mrs. Ivory
has often scheduled 7 A.M. meetings with families
when this was the only time they could be seen.

Officially, the day's schedule begins at 8 A.M. And a
"routine day" taken from Mrs. Ivory's calendar goes
like this:

8:00–8:30 A.M.

Met with two teachers at Roosevelt School—one
conference in regard to an 8-year-old exhibiting behavior problems and the other to discuss purchase
of a pair of shoes for a needy child in special-
education class. A shoe fund in the school system
permits purchase of shoes so that no child need be
absent because of this deprivation.

8:45 A.M.

Stopped at the Church of the Brethren to see the
assistant minister about a basket of groceries being
contributed to a family facing an emergency situation: The father is ill and temporarily unemployed.

The situation was first discovered by the social worker's contact with the children in school.

9:00 A.M.

Gave a talk to a high-school group called Future Teachers on "The Role of a School Social Worker." Answered questions after presentation and made appointments for students who want to discuss a social-work career.

10:05 A.M.

Held a supervisory conference with an attendance worker on some of his cases. Included a coffee break during this time, but brought coffee to desk during meeting. Three telephone calls interrupted the conference; all had to do with current cases, but had to discontinue all calls until 11 A.M. when conference with attendance worker finished.

11:10 A.M.

Reviewed telephone messages and returned calls. Made five other calls to families. One was concerning attendance of children in school; another had to do with a job referral; another concerned emotional problems of a child and the recommendation that he be referred to the child-guidance clinic; the fourth and fifth calls had to do with clients of the Department of Public Welfare and ways in which school social services could help them.

12:00 Noon

Made three home calls, since many parents can be seen only during the lunch hour due to their work

schedules. The problems were varied: clothing needs; inability to pay book rentals; a misunderstanding about a school policy on bus transport.
12:40 P.M.

Stopped at a business establishment. The owner gave social worker a check for $113.00 to pay for a Head Start child in a nursery school program. Some of the Head Start children had not been recommended for kindergarten because of immaturity; they needed more "readiness" work than the summer program provided and were placed in nursery-school programs on scholarships. This businessman had volunteered to sponsor a child.
12:45–1:30 P.M.

Lunch. Read social-work journals and recorded notes on cases during this time.
1:30–3:40 P.M.

Read mail regarding social-work meeting, case conferences with other agencies, announcement of new literature in the field, an invitation to a conference on social work, request for verification of enrollment of a student, letters from former students who were problems and are now in group counseling. Returned and made telephone calls.
Saw a parent who dropped in to inquire about clothing she needs for her family. Helped her make selections from clothing room where donations are stored. Clothing is collected in school drives, is donated by individuals, churches, stores and clean-

ers who turn over unclaimed items left months beyond the holding date. A young male adult asked for help to get a job, and was referred to an agency that could be of assistance.

4:05 P.M.

Returned from slight break to have conference with director of Pupil Personnel and Guidance, a school counselor and a parent, regarding her son, Jimmy. The counselor had been working with the boy because of his behavior problems and his failing grades despite an apparent ability to achieve. The director gave Jimmy a psychological test, then later discussed the results and made plans with all concerned to meet the child's needs.

5:10 P.M.

On the way home stopped at two homes regarding problems that could not be taken care of earlier due to lack of time—the day is never long enough!

7:00–9:00 P.M.

Attended parent group meeting. This interracial group is an outgrowth or continuation of parent groups that a social worker initiated during the summer Head Start program. The speaker for the evening was a school principal who explained about individual differences in children and how the school is trying to provide situations and experiences geared to these differences and individual needs and abilities through a "staggered day" program. The pupils arrive and leave in 'stag-

gered' groups so that there is time for individualized instruction and small-group projects, during
the periods when the entire student body is not
present. The parents discuss the program enthusi-
astically, and several cite instances of achievement
in their children. Previously this group of parents
had been most antagonistic or apathetic about the
school or education. These meetings are meant to
bring the home and school closer together.
About 10:00 P.M.

Home. Kick off the shoes. Relax . . . But at the
same time plan for tomorrow . . .

Does it make you tired just to read about the day
of a social worker in the public-schoool setting? It
seems like a staggering work load, but, again, this is
the very thing—the discipline of hard work—which
so many practitioners extol. They do not expect their
profession to be a soft touch, and the rewards in this
setting, as in other social-service areas, cannot be
measured against the time and effort involved. Seeing youngsters and their families improve their social relationships and gain understanding about and
work toward their potential is something that has to
be experienced to be appreciated. At any rate, it is
evident by now that, if you become a social worker,
there is little chance you will be a victim of the modern "disease" *ennui*. There is no time for boredom!

16
WHAT'S AHEAD? . . .

Plenty! "Boundless horizons" is the term used to describe the future of social work in much of the published material sent out by social-service and professional social-work organizations. Being in on the "new" is always exciting, and this is very much a part of social work.

"Vast new areas are opening up for persons interested in problems of urbanization," says Cathryn Guyler, director of NCSWC, "and industry is just beginning to utilize the knowledge and skills of social workers." She adds: "What excites [young people] about social-work careers is a chance to engage actively in the large and pertinent issues of the day" such as urban problems and the human-rights movement.

Social service will be in the future, as it has been in the 1960's, for the *"now* generation" and for people who want to do something useful with their lives.

Devising improvements and directions for social-welfare policy is an area of activity social workers will be increasingly involved in. Future social workers will be called in as specialists for broad governmental and voluntary programs in all phases of service, including international social-welfare programs and domestic public assistance.

There are now over 8.6 million people receiving aid from United States government sources. One in every twenty-three persons lacks the income needed to meet minimal living expenses, and that number is increasing. This means costs of public assistance are rising, and the subject is highly controversial. It was debated strongly and avidly in the 90th Congress during 1967 and its second session in 1968. The debates on how to get people off relief roles and help them become self-supporting will continue. Social workers will be needed to assist with this pressing problem.

"Labor Department surveys show that the unemployment rate in our ghettos—measuring joblessness, nonparticipation in the labor force and earnings below the poverty line—averages 34 percent; the most serious unemployment problem today is among nonwhite teenagers, where it averages 30 percent," said United States Senator Jacob Javits in August

1967. So here is another area where social workers will be needed in the days and years ahead.

Whitney M. Young Jr., Executive Director of the National Urban League, is most concerned about unemployment among Negro youth and feels the entire social-work field needs many more members of all minority groups in its career ranks.

There is an increasing demand "for services to the minorities among us," Mr. Young points out. "Yet—unhappily—it is possible for fewer and fewer members of the ruling majority to empathize, even to communicate, with the disadvantaged. Because of this, we must develop the potential for leadership within the ghetto itself."

This means not only encouraging, with financial aid, etc., Negro, Puerto Rican and other minority youth to become professional social workers, but also to pull these young people in on other levels of training. The 1966 congressional act which made $70 million available for training and employing the unskilled for public-service jobs is a start in this direction. Unless there is a concerted effort to include a representative number of minority youth in the new social-service programs, much valuable manpower will be lost.

Mr. Young warns, though, that the subprofessional or technician or "welfare intern"—no matter what his racial or cultural background—"must not find that he has entered a dead-end street. Routine simple tasks suffice at first, but the novitiate period must lead to the aide level—direct service to clients—and then to the semiprofessional level, with widened responsibility and scope, and with rising pay along the way."

Recruitment for social work among all kinds of youth is a future job area for many social workers, and you might find your niche here. Extensive and well-organized programs will be needed, with public relations and informational campaigns concomitant elements.

Undergraduate education in social welfare will have a great deal more emphasis in the years ahead. If you plan to enter the academic field of social work, you could be involved in establishing criteria for an undergraduate social-welfare curriculum. Or maybe you will help set up new programs in conjunction with schools of social work. Or you might develop new teaching materials and curriculum guides to be used to prepare college students who want to enter a social-service career directly after graduation.

There will be a need for future researchers to study social work manpower "in order to identify both the numbers and kinds of personnel needed to staff the social-welfare services found necessary and to pinpoint the causes and cures of manpower shortages so that appropriate staff may be recruited and retained," states the Task Force Report of the Department of Health, Education and Welfare. It notes also that research in the Department itself, in universities and in responsible social-service agencies "would make possible . . . the prediction of future needs with greater accuracy."

You might, in the years ahead, be involved in community social-welfare planning that will have to do with *specialized* problems, not necessarily an overall social-service program. Hospital development, mental-health programs, antipoverty projects, comprehensive health centers could require individualized concentrated organization and planning.

New methods of funding welfare programs might be another field requiring attention from social-service career people. This could include intensive work in community involvement—getting grass roots action and finding ways to motivate the poor.

Poverty programs will need social workers for many years, because the causes of poverty do not disappear by themselves.

"Social workers are the front-line troops in our war on poverty," said President Lyndon B. Johnson in 1967. "They treat the social ills of society as the physician treats its physical ills. Our nation needs their valuable help . . . and this need will grow as our society undergoes the changes that inevitably accompany progress."

So what's ahead? Opportunity, challenge, significant and vital work, self-fulfillment—in short, a career with a purpose.

SUGGESTED FURTHER READING

The following books will help you to learn more about careers in social service:

Aid to Dependent Children, Winifred Bell. New York and London: Columbia University Press.

Careers in Social Work, Frances A. Koestler. New York: Henry Z. Walck.

Child Welfare, Principles and Methods, Dorothy Zietz. New York: John Wiley & Sons, Inc.

Community Welfare Organization, Principles & Practices, Arthur Dunham. New York: Thomas Y. Crowell Company.

Concepts and Methods of Social Work, Walter A. Friedlander, ed. New Jersey: Prentice-Hall, Inc.

Encyclopedia of Social Work, Harry L. Lurie, ed. NASW, New York.

Field of Social Work, The, 3rd ed., Arthur E. Fink, Everett E. Wilson, Merrill B. Conover. New York: Henry Holt & Company.

Group Methods in the Public Welfare Program, Norman Fenton, Ph.D., and Kermit T. Wiltse, D.S.W., eds. Palo Alto, California: Pacific Books.

Groups in Guidance, Edward C. Glanz. Boston: Allyn and Bacon, Inc.

Industrial Society and Social Welfare, Harold L. Wilensky and Charles N. Lebeaux. New York: Russell Sage Foundation.

In-Service Casework Training, Elizabeth Nicholds. New York and London: Columbia University Press.

Introduction to Social Welfare, 2nd ed., Walter A. Friedlander. New Jersey: Prentice-Hall, Inc.

New Careers for the Poor, Arthur Pearl and Frank Riessman. New York: The Free Press.

Opportunities in Foreign Service, Lucille Harrigan. New York: Universal Publishing Company.

Religion and Social Work, F. Ernest Johnson, ed. New York: Harper & Bros.

Social Group Work, Gisela Konopka. New Jersey: Prentice-Hall, Inc.

Social Welfare Forum, The. New York and London: Columbia University Press.

Social Work: an Introduction to the Field, Herbert Hewitt Stroup. New York: American Book Company.

Social Worker, Margaret Williamson. New York: The Macmillan Company.

So You Want to be a Social Worker, Helen Harris Perlman. New York: Harper & Row Publishing Company, Inc.

Toward Public Understanding of Casework, Viola Paradise. New York: Russell Sage Foundation.

Trends in Social Work, Frank J. Bruno. New York: Columbia University Press.

APPENDIX I

TERMS FOR SOCIAL WORK POSITIONS

EXECUTIVE AND
SUPERVISORY

Social welfare administrator
Casework director

Community-organization director
Community-planning director
Planning director

Appendix I

Research director
Social-welfare director

Casework supervisor
Child-welfare supervisor
Community supervisor
Community-organization supervisor
District supervisor
Group-work supervisor
Homemaker supervisor
Social-welfare supervisor

GROUP WORK AREA

Day-care aide
Detached street worker
Golden-age worker
Group-work aide
Program aide
Social-group worker
Training aide
Youth worker

CASEWORK AREA

Adoption worker
Adult worker
Aide to the aged
Baby sitting and child service
Case consultant
Case finder
Case reviewer
Caseworker
Casework aide
Child-care worker

Child-placement worker
Child-welfare assistant
Child-welfare consultant
Child-welfare worker
Community case aide
Correctional aide
DPW consultant
Economic aide
Employment aide
Employment interviewer
Employment worker
Family counselor
Family-service worker
Foster-home finder
Foster-home worker
Home-economics aide
Home economist
Home–school visitor
Home visitor
Household helper
Homemaker
Home aide
Institutional social worker
Intake worker
Intensive social worker
Occupational rehabilitation counselor
Parole officer
Probation officer
Relocation aide
Social-welfare technician
Training aide
Welfare assistant

177

COMMUNITY
ORGANIZATION AND
PLANNING

Administrative aide
Assistant coordinator
Assistant extension worker
Community-action aide
Community agent
Community consultant
Community-organization assistant
Community-organization worker

Community worker
Neighborhood coordinator
Neighborhood worker
Neighborhood youth worker
Planning associate
Planning assistant
School–community agent

RESEARCH

Research assistant
Research associate
Research worker
Statistical assistant

APPENDIX II

COLLEGES AND UNIVERSITIES OFFERING UNDER-
GRADUATE COURSES WITH SOCIAL WELFARE CONTENT

Alabama College, Montevallo, Alabama 35115
Huntingdon College, Montgomery, Alabama 36106
Spring Hill College, Mobile, Alabama 36608

University of Alaska, College, Alaska 99701

Arizona State University, Tempe, Arizona 85281
The University of Arizona, Tucson, Arizona 85721

Arkansas State University, State College, Arkansas 72467
University of Arkansas, Fayetteville, Arkansas 72701

California State College at Hayward, Hayward, California 94542
California State College at Long Beach, Long Beach, California 90804

Appendix II

California State College at Los Angeles, Los Angeles, California
90032

Chapman College, Orange, California 92666

Chico State College, Chico, California 95927

College of Notre Dame, Belmont, California 94002

Fresno State College, Fresno, California 93726

Humboldt State College, Arcata, California 95521

La Sierra College, Riverside, California 92505

Pepperdine College, Los Angeles, California 90044

Sacramento State College, Sacramento, California 95819

San Diego State College, San Diego, California 92115

San Francisco College for Women, San Francisco, California
94118

San Francisco State College, San Francisco, California 94132

San Jose State College, San Jose, California 95114

University of California, Berkeley, California 94720

University of California, Los Angeles, California 90024

University of San Francisco, San Francisco, California 94117

University of the Pacific, Stockton, California 95204

Whittier College, Whittier, California 90608

University of Denver, Denver, Colorado 80210

Central Connecticut State College, New Britain, Connecticut
06050

Southern Connecticut State College, New Haven, Connecticut
06510

The Catholic University of America, Washington, D. C. 20017

Florida State University, Tallahassee, Florida 32306

University of Florida, Gainesville, Florida 32601

The Fort Valley State College, Fort Valley, Georgia 31030

Georgia State College, Atlanta, Georgia 30303

University of Georgia, Athens, Georgia 30602

Boise College, Boise, Idaho 83701

Idaho State University, Pocatello, Idaho 83201

University of Idaho, Moscow, Idaho 83843

Augustana College, Rock Island, Illinois 61202
George Williams College, Downers Grove, Illinois 60515
Illinois Wesleyan University, Bloomington, Illinois 61701
Roosevelt University, Chicago, Illinois 60605
Southern Illinois University, Carbondale, Illinois 62903
Southern Illinois University, Edwardsville, Illinois 62025
University of Illinois, Urbana, Illinois 61801
Wheaton College, Wheaton, Illinois 60187

Anderson College, Anderson, Indiana 46012
Ball State University, Muncie, Indiana 47306
Goshen College, Goshen, Indiana 46526
Indiana State University, Terre Haute, Indiana 47809
Indiana University, Bloomington, Indiana 47401
St. Francis College, Fort Wayne, Indiana 46808
Taylor University, Upland, Indiana 46989
Valparaiso University, Valparaiso, Indiana 46383

Clarke College, Dubuque, Iowa 52001
Drake University, Des Moines, Iowa 50311
Morningside College, Sioux City, Iowa 51106
The University of Iowa, Iowa City, Iowa 52240
Wartburg College, Waverly, Iowa 50677

Washburn University, Topeka, Kansas 66621
Wichita State University, Wichita, Kansas 67208

Catherine Spalding College, Louisville, Kentucky 40203
Eastern Kentucky University, Richmond, Kentucky 40475
Morehead State University, Morehead, Kentucky 40351
University of Kentucky, Lexington, Kentucky 40506
Villa Madonna College, Covington, Kentucky 41012
Western Kentucky University, Bowling Green, Kentucky 42101

University of Maine, Orono, Maine 04473

College of Notre Dame of Maryland, Baltimore, Maryland 21210
Hood College, Frederick, Maryland 21701

Appendix II

St. Joseph College, Emmitsburg, Maryland 21727
University of Maryland, College Park, Maryland 20740

American International College, Springfield, Massachusetts 01109
Eastern Nazarene College, Wollaston, Massachusetts 02170
Our Lady of the Elms College, Chicopee, Massachusetts 01013

Albion College, Albion, Michigan 49224
Alma College, Alma, Michigan 48801
Andrews University, Berrien Springs, Michigan 49104
Eastern Michigan University, Ypsilanti, Michigan 48197
Kalamazoo College, Kalamazoo, Michigan 49001
Marygrove College, Detroit, Michigan 48221
Mercy College of Detroit, Detroit, Michigan 48219
Michigan State University, East Lansing, Michigan 48823
Northern Michigan University, Marquette, Michigan 49855
University of Detroit, Detroit, Michigan 48221
University of Michigan, Ann Arbor, Michigan 48104
Western Michigan University, Kalamazoo, Michigan 49045

Augsburg College, Minneapolis, Minnesota 55404
Bethel College, St. Paul, Minnesota 55101
Carleton College, Northfield, Minnesota 55057
College of St. Scholastica, Duluth, Minnesota 55811
Concordia College, Moorhead, Minnesota 56560
Gustavus Adolphus College, St. Peter, Minnesota 56082
Hamline University, St. Paul, Minnesota 55101
Moorhead State College, Moorhead, Minnesota 56560
St. Olaf College, Northfield, Minnesota 55057
University of Minnesota, Minneapolis, Minnesota 55455
University of Minnesota, Duluth, Minnesota 44812
University of Minnesota, Morris, Minnesota 56267

Mississippi State College for Women, Columbus, Mississippi
     39701
Mississippi State University, State College, Mississippi 39762

Marillac College, St. Louis, Missouri 63121
University of Missouri, Columbia, Missouri 65201

University of Montana, Missoula, Montana 59801

The Creighton University, Omaha, Nebraska 68131
Dana College, Blair, Nebraska 68008
Nebraska Wesleyan University, Lincoln, Nebraska 68504
University of Omaha, Omaha, Nebraska 68101

University of Nevada, Reno, Nevada 89507

University of New Hampshire, Durham, New Hampshire 03824

Rutgers, The State University, New Brunswick, New Jersey 08901
Upsala College, East Orange, New Jersey 07019

New Mexico State University, Las Cruces, New Mexico 88001

Adelphi University, Garden City, L. I., New York 11530
The City College of the City University of New York, New York, New York 10031
D'Youville College, Buffalo, New York 14201
Elmira College, Elmira, New York 14901
Hunter College, New York, New York 10021
Keuka College, Keuka Park, New York 14478
Nazareth College of Rochester, Rochester, New York 14610
New York University, New York, New York 10003
Queens College, Flushing, New York 11367
Rosary Hill College, Buffalo, New York 14226
St. Bernadine of Siena College, Loudonville, New York 12211
Skidmore College, Saratoga Springs, New York 12866
State University of New York, Buffalo, New York 14214
Syracuse University, Syracuse, New York 13210
Utica College of Syracuse University, Utica, New York 13502
Wagner College, Staten Island, New York 10301

Lenoir Rhyne College, Hickory, North Carolina 28601
St. Augustine's College, Raleigh, North Carolina 27602
University of North Carolina, Greensboro, North Carolina 27412

University of North Dakota, Grand Forks, North Dakota 58202

Bowling Green State University, Bowling Green, Ohio 43402
Capital University, Columbus, Ohio 43209
Central State University, Wilberforce, Ohio 45384
College of St. Mary of the Springs, Columbus, Ohio 43219
College of Wooster, Wooster, Ohio 44691
Kent State University, Kent, Ohio 44240
Miami University, Oxford, Ohio 45056
Ohio Northern University, Ada, Ohio 45810
Ohio State University, Columbus, Ohio 43210
Ohio University, Athens, Ohio 45701
Ohio Wesleyan University, Delaware, Ohio 43015
Our Lady of Cincinnati College, Cincinnati, Ohio 45206
University of Akron, Akron, Ohio 44304
University of Cincinnati, Cincinnati, Ohio 45221
University of Dayton, Dayton, Ohio 45409
University of Toledo, Toledo, Ohio 43606
Youngstown University, Youngstown, Ohio 44503

Northwestern State College, Alva, Oklahoma 73717
University of Tulsa, Tulsa, Oklahoma 74104

Mount Angel College, Mount Angel, Oregon 97362
University of Oregon, Eugene, Oregon 97403

Albright College, Reading, Pennsylvania 19604
Beaver College, Glenside, Pennsylvania 19038
La Salle College, Philadelphia, Pennsylvania 19141
Mercyhurst College, Erie, Pennsylvania 16501
Muhlenberg College, Allentown, Pennsylvania 18104
Pennsylvania State University, University Park, Pennsylvania 16802
St. Francis College, Loretto, Pennsylvania 15940
Temple University, Philadelphia, Pennsylvania 19122
University of Scranton, Scranton, Pennsylvania 18510
Villa Maria College, Erie, Pennsylvania 16505

Inter American University, San German, Puerto Rico 00753

Barrington College, Barrington, Rhode Island 02806

Newberry College, Newberry, South Carolina 29108
Winthrop College, Rock Hill, South Carolina 29730

Augustana College, Sioux Falls, South Dakota 57102
Mount Marty College, Yankton, South Dakota 57078
Sioux Falls College, Sioux Falls, South Dakota 57101
University of South Dakota, Vermillion, South Dakota 57069

East Tennessee State University, Johnson City, Tennessee 37602
Knoxville College, Knoxville, Tennessee 37921
Tennessee State University, Nashville, Tennessee 37203
University of Chattanooga, Chattanooga, Tennessee 37403
University of Tennessee, Knoxville, Tennessee 37916

Baylor University, Waco, Texas 76703
Prairie View Agricultural and Mechanical College, Prairie View,
    Texas 77445
Texas Woman's University, Denton, Texas 76204
University of Texas, Austin, Texas 78712

University of Utah, Salt Lake City, Utah 84112
Utah State University, Logan, Utah 84321
Weber State College, Ogden, Utah 84403

Trinity College, Burlington, Vermont 05401

Hollins College, Hollins College, Virginia 24020
Lynchburg College, Lynchburg, Virginia 24505
Madison College, Harrisonburg, Virginia 22802
Norfolk State College, Norfolk, Virginia 23504
University of Virginia, Fredericksburg, Virginia 22401

Eastern Washington State College, Cheney, Washington 99004
Pacific Lutheran University, Tacoma, Washington 98447
Seattle Pacific College, Seattle, Washington 98119
University of Washington, Seattle, Washington 98105
Washington State University, Pullman, Washington 99163

West Virginia Wesleyan College, Buckhannon, West Virginia
    26201

Mount Mary College, Milwaukee, Wisconsin 53222
University of Wisconsin, Madison, Wisconsin 53706
University of Wisconsin, Milwaukee, Wisconsin 53211
Wisconsin State University, La Crosse, Wisconsin 54601
Wisconsin State University, Whitewater, Wisconsin 53190

APPENDIX III

GRADUATE PROFESSIONAL SCHOOLS OF SOCIAL WORK

CANADA

University of British Columbia
    School of Social Work
    Vancouver, British Columbia
    Dr. George M. Hougham,
    Acting Director
University of Manitoba
    School of Social Work
    Winnipeg, Manitoba
    Helen Mann, Director
Carleton University School of Social Work
    St. Patrick's Campus
    Echo Drive
    Ottawa, Ontario

    Rev. Swithun Bowers, Director
University of Toronto
    School of Social Work
    Toronto, Ontario
    Charles E. Hendry, Director
Laval University
    School of Social Work
    Quebec, Quebec
    Nicolas Zay, Director
McGill University
    School of Social Work
    Montreal, Quebec
    David E. Woodsworth, Director

UNITED STATES

Arizona State University
    Graduate School of Social Service Administration
    Tempe, Arizona 85281

    Horace W. Lundberg, Dean
University of California
    School of Social Welfare
    Berkeley, California 94720

Milton Chernin, Dean
University of California
School of Social Welfare
Los Angeles, California
90024
Eileen Blackey, Dean
Fresno State College
Division of Social Work
Fresno, California 93726
Thomas M. Brigham, Director
Sacramento State College
School of Social Work
Sacramento, California
95819
Alan D. Wade, Dean
San Diego State College
School of Social Work
San Diego, California 92115
Ernest F. Witte, Dean
University of Southern California School of Social Work
Los Angeles, California
90007
Malcolm B. Stinson, Dean
University of Denver
The Graduate School of Social Work
Denver, Colorado 80210
Emil M. Sunley, Dean
University of Connecticut
School of Social Work
West Hartford, Connecticut
06119
Harleigh B. Trecker, Dean
The Catholic University of America
The National Catholic School of Social Work
Washington, D. C. 20017
Frederick J. Ferris, Dean

Howard University
School of Social Work
Washington, D. C. 20001
Mary Ella Robertson, Dean
Florida State University
Graduate Department of Social Work
Tallahassee, Florida 32306
Margaret C. Bristol, Acting Chairman
Atlanta University
School of Social Work
Atlanta, Georgia 30314
William S. Jackson, Dean
University of Georgia
School of Social Work
Athens, Georgia 30601
Charles A. Stewart, Dean
University of Hawaii
School of Social Work
Honolulu, Hawaii 96822
Fred DelliQuadri, Dean
University of Chicago
School of Social Service Administration
Chicago, Illinois 60637
Alton A. Linford, Dean
University of Illinois
The Jane Addams Graduate School of Social Work
Urbana, Illinois 61801
Mark Hale, Director
Loyola University
School of Social Work
Chicago, Illinois 60611
Matthew H. Schoenbaum, Dean
Indiana University
Graduate School of Social Service
Indianapolis, Indiana 46204

Appendix III

Richard G. Lawrence, Dean
The University of Iowa
School of Social Work
Iowa City, Iowa 52240
Frank Z. Glick, Director
University of Kansas
Graduate Department of Social Work
Lawrence, Kansas 66044
Joseph F. Meisels, Chairman
University of Louisville
The Raymond A. Kent School of Social Work
Louisville, Kentucky 40208
Kenneth W. Kindelsperger, Dean
Louisiana State University
School of Social Welfare
Baton Rouge, Louisiana 70803
Earl E. Klein, Director
Tulane University
School of Social Work
New Orleans, Louisiana 70118
Walter L. Kindelsperger, Dean
University of Maryland
School of Social Work
Baltimore, Maryland 21201
Daniel Thursz, Dean
Boston College
School of Social Work
Boston, Massachusetts 02116
Rev. John V. Driscoll, S. J., Dean
Boston University
School of Social Work
Boston, Massachusetts 02215
Simmons College

School of Social Work
Boston, Massachusetts 02116
Robert F. Rutherford, Director
Smith College
School for Social Work
Northampton, Massachusetts 01060
Howard J. Parad, Dean
Michigan State University
School of Social Work
East Lansing, Michigan 48823
Gwen Andrew, Acting Director
University of Michigan
School of Social Work
Ann Arbor, Michigan 48104
Fedele F. Fauri, Dean
Wayne State University
School of Social Work
Detroit, Michigan 48202
Sidney Dillick, Dean
University of Minnesota
School of Social Work
Minneapolis, Minnesota 55455
John C. Kidneigh, Director
University of Missouri
The School of Social Work
Columbia, Missouri 65202
Arthur J. Robins, Director
St. Louis University
School of Social Service
St. Louis, Missouri 63108
Rev. B. J. Coughlin, S. J., Dean
Washington University
The George Warren Brown School of Social Work
St. Louis, Missouri 63130

Wayne Vasey, Dean
University of Nebraska
Graduate School of Social
Work
Lincoln, Nebraska 68508
Richard Guilford, Director
Rutgers, The State University
Graduate School of Social
Work
New Brunswick, New Jersey
08903
Werner W. Boehm, Dean
Adelphi University
School of Social Work
Garden City, Long Island,
New York 11530
Joseph L. Vigilante, Dean
Columbia University
School of Social Work
New York, New York 10028
Sidney Berengarten, Acting
Dean
Fordham University
School of Social Service
New York, New York 10016
James R. Dumpson, Dean
Hunter College of the City Uni-
versity of New York
School of Social Work
New York, New York 10021
Paul Schreiber, Dean
New York University
Graduate School of Social
Work
New York, New York 10003
Alex Rosen, Dean
State University of New York
at Buffalo
School of Social Welfare
Buffalo, New York 14214
Benjamin H. Lyndon, Dean

Syracuse University (New York)
School of Social Work
Syracuse, New York 13210
Walter M. Beattie, Jr., Dean
Yeshiva University
Wurzweiler School of Social
Work
New York, New York 10003
Morton I. Teicher, Dean
University of North Carolina
School of Social Work
Chapel Hill, North Carolina
27514
C. Wilson Anderson, Dean
Ohio State University
School of Social Work
Columbus, Ohio 43210
Richard Medhurst, Director
Cincinnati Center of Ohio State
University
University of Cincinnati
Cincinnati, Ohio 45219
Case Western Reserve University
School of Applied Social
Sciences
Cleveland, Ohio 44106
Herman D. Stein, Dean
University of Oklahoma
School of Social Work
Norman, Oklahoma 73069
C. Stanley Clifton, Director
Portland State College
School of Social Work
Portland, Oregon 97207
Gordon Hearn, Dean
Bryn Mawr College
Carola Woerishoffer Gradu-
ate Department of Social
Work and Social Research
Bryn Mawr, Pennsylvania
19010

Appendix III

Katherine D. Lower, Director
University of Pennsylvania
School of Social Work
Philadelphia, Pennsylvania
19103
John S. Morgan, Dean
University of Pittsburgh
Graduate School of Social
Work
Pittsburgh, Pennsylvania
15213
William H. McCullough,
Dean
University of Puerto Rico
School of Social Work
Rio Piedras, Puerto Rico
00753
Rosa C. Marin, Director
The University of Tennessee
School of Social Work
Nashville, Tennessee 37203
Sue Spencer, Director
Our Lady of the Lake College
The Worden School of Social Service
San Antonio, Texas 78207
Sister Mary Immaculate, Director
The University of Texas
Graduate School of Social
Work

Austin, Texas 78712
Jack Otis, Director
University of Utah
Graduate School of Social
Work
Salt Lake City, Utah 84112
Rex A. Skidmore, Dean
Richmond Professional Institute
School of Social Work
Richmond, Virginia 23220
Richard Lodge, Dean
University of Washington
School of Social Work
Seattle, Washington 98105
Charles B. Brink, Dean
West Virginia University
Division of Social Work
Morgantown, West Virginia
26506
Bernhard Scher, Director
University of Wisconsin
Madison, School of Social
Work
Madison, Wisconsin 53706
Martin B. Loeb, Director
University of Wisconsin
Milwaukee, School of Social
Work
Milwaukee, Wisconsin 53201
Quentin F. Schenk, Dean

INDEX

Index

Pope Paul VI, 154
poverty, early ideas on, 22-25; early attempts to cope with, 25-27
probation, 116, 117, 119, 121
probation officer, *see* social worker, corrections
Protestant World Council of Churches, 146
psychiatrist, 105, 106, 107
psychologist (clinical), 105, 106
psychotherapy, 107
Public Health Service, U.S., National Institute of Mental Health, 111

Rath, Alfred M., 156
Red Cross, 18, 75, 76, 83, 106, 152
rehabilitation, 115, 116, 129, 146
Riessman, Frank, 85
Right to Be Different, The, 161
Rivera, Julio, 14
Rockefeller Brothers Fund, 137
Russell Sage Foundation, 137

San Francisco Suicide Prevention (SFSP), 12-13
Scott, George C., 28
Selling, Carolyn, 139, 140
settlement workers, *see* community organization
Shriver, R. Sargent, 128
Smith, Paula, 11
social service, careers in, 12-20, 29, 56-59, 62-68, 71-80, 92, 171-176; religious, 18, 152, 153, 154, 155-163; overseas, 18-19, 145-154; educational preparation for, 34-45, 59, 79, 139, 140, 141, 174; paid training in, 46-55; research in, 136-138, 141
social worker, 13, 14, 16; demand for, 19, 71-80, 175-176; salaries of, 20, 62, 71, 73, 74, 88, 92, 130; stereotype of, 21-22; history of, 22; essential qualities of, 29-33, 44-45;

democratic values of, 38-39; duties of, 57-60, 62-70, 92-101, 164-170; family oriented, 92-101; psychiatric, 102-109, 111-112, 141, 142; correctional, 113-122; private, 143-144; administrative, 138-140
social-work technician, 173-174
Stern, Henry B., 64
Stevenson, Adlai E., III, 127, 128
Stroup, Herbert H., 38
Sublett, Samuel, 12
Sullivan, Monroe B., 29

Thompson, Mike, 68-70
Thomsen, Moritz, 151, 152
Toynbee Hall (London), 27
Traveler's Aid Society, 12, 18, 77, 83, 84
Tri-Faith Service, 29

Unitarian-Universalist Service Committee, 18, 19
United Community Services, 68, 69, 130
United Nations, 19, 146; Department of Economic and Social Affairs, 145; UNICEF, 146, 147
United Neighborhood Houses, 125
United Presbyterian Church, 157
United Fund Campaign, 69
University of the Pacific, 13

Veterans Administration, 59, 89, 106
visiting homemaker services, 86
Volunteers in Service to America (VISTA), 28, 46-48

Welfare Council of Metropolitan Chicago, 89
Work-Study Program, *see* Federal Work-Study Program

Young, Whitney M., Jr., 173
YMCA, 14, 18, 63
YWCA, 61, 62